T0304374

THE OFFICIAL GRAPHIC NOVEL

SPORTS VOL. #1
SUPERHEROES
STEPHEN CURRY

To Megan, Zach, and Max . . . you are my superheroes
(sorry, it was right there!)—JB

For Ella, Oscar, and Kim—my favorite superheroes,
villains, and jokers!—RK

PENGUIN WORKSHOP
An imprint of Penguin Random House LLC, New York

First published in the United States of America by Penguin Workshop,
an imprint of Penguin Random House LLC, New York, 2024

Unanimous
Publishing

Text copyright © 2024 by Joshua Bycel, Richard Korson, and Unanimous Media Holdings, LLC
Illustrations copyright © 2024 by Unanimous Media Holdings, LLC
Creative Direction by Erick Peyton
Content Editor Kalyna Maria Kutny
Design by Mary Claire Cruz

Visit us online at penguinrandomhouse.com.

Library of Congress Control Number: 2024942243

Manufactured in China

ISBN 9780593382462 (pbk)   10 9 8 7 6 5 4 3 2 TOPL
ISBN 9780593382486 (hc)   10 9 8 7 6 5 4 3 2 TOPL

This is a work of nonfiction narrated by fictional characters. The events that unfold in the
narrative are rooted in historical fact. Some characters have been created and the dialogue of
some historical figures has been fictionalized in service of the narrative.

THE OFFICIAL GRAPHIC NOVEL

SPORTS VOL. #1
SUPERHEROES
STEPHEN CURRY

BY **JOSH BYCEL** AND **RICH KORSON**

ILLUSTRATED BY **DAMION SCOTT**

LETTERING BY **HASSAN OTSMANE-ELHAOU**

Unanimous
Publishing

Penguin Workshop

CHAPTER ONE

THE SPORTS SUPERHEROES

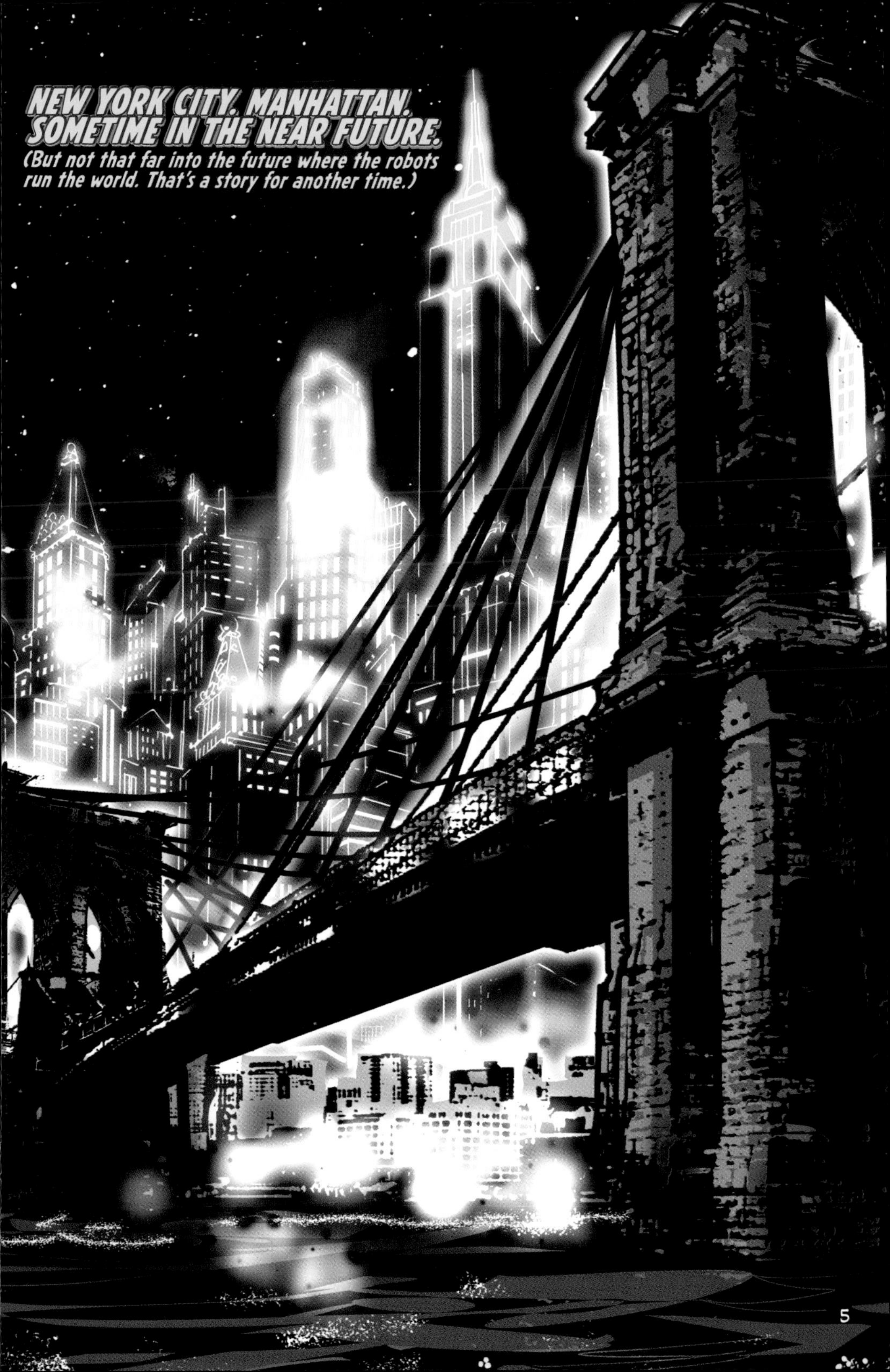
NEW YORK CITY. MANHATTAN. SOMETIME IN THE NEAR FUTURE.
(But not that far into the future where the robots run the world. That's a story for another time.)

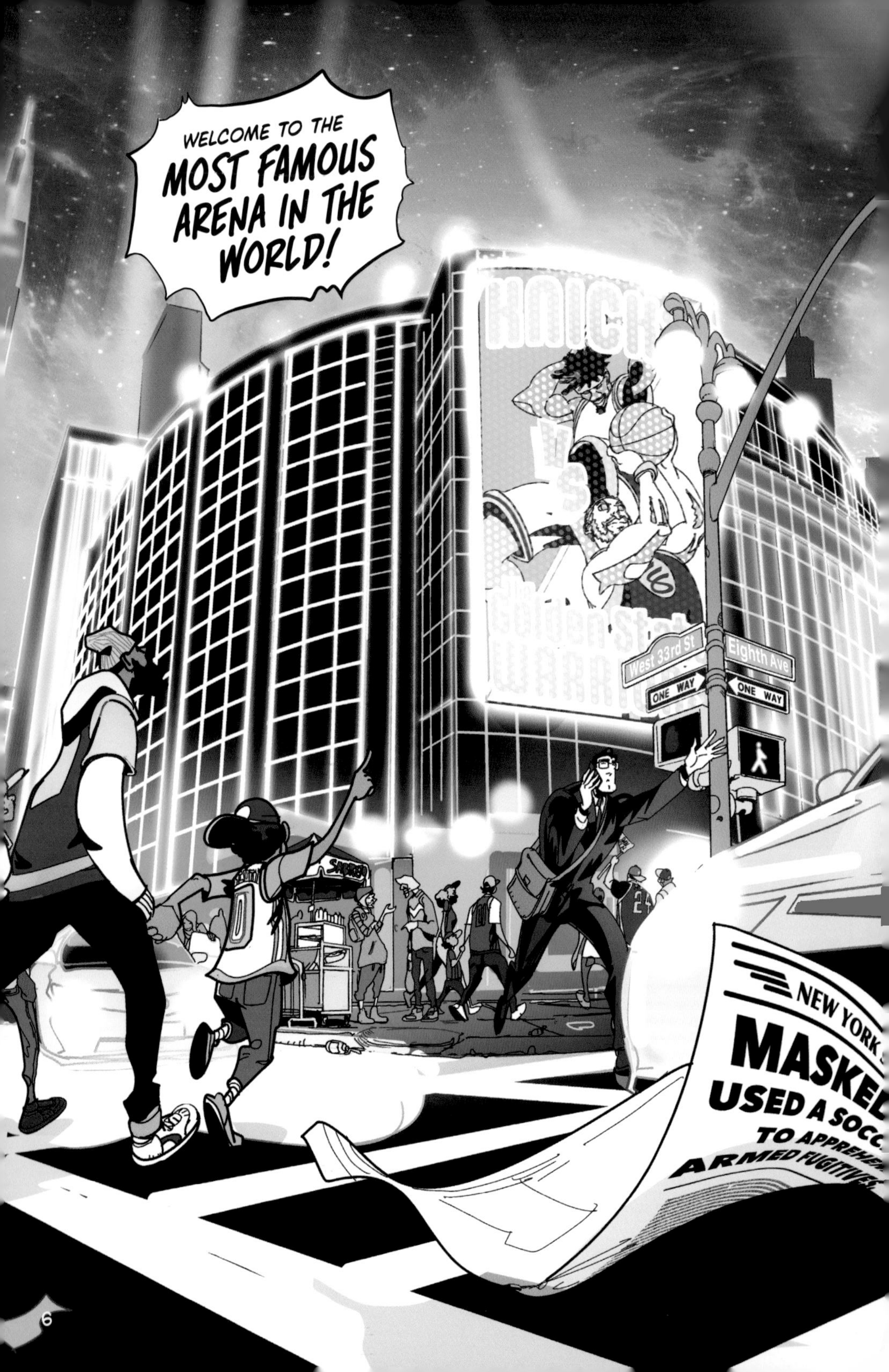
WELCOME TO THE MOST FAMOUS ARENA IN THE WORLD!
West 33rd St
Eighth Ave
ONE WAY
ONE WAY

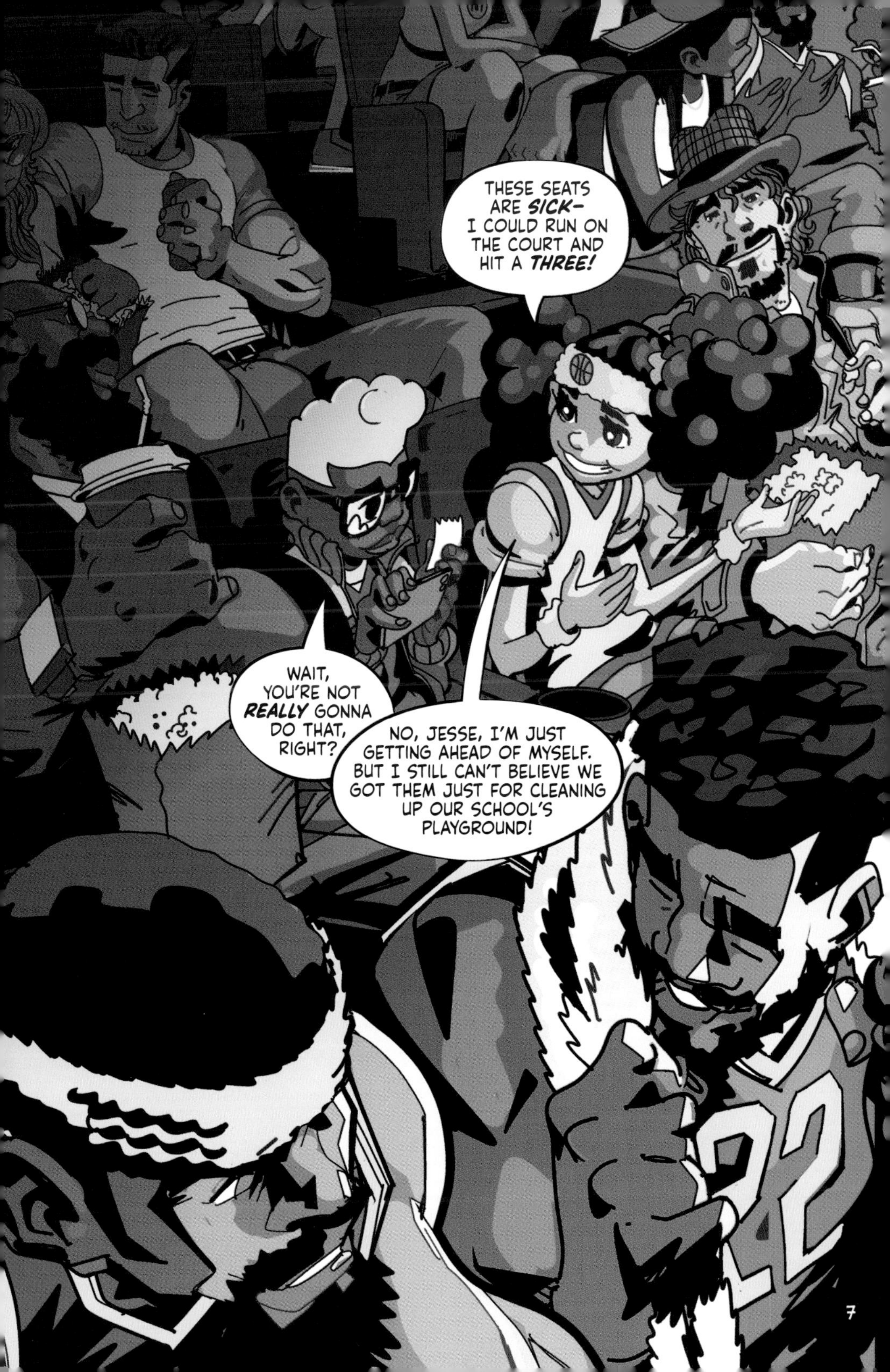
THESE SEATS ARE SICK– I COULD RUN ON THE COURT AND HIT A THREE!
WAIT, YOU'RE NOT REALLY GONNA DO THAT, RIGHT?
NO, JESSE, I'M JUST GETTING AHEAD OF MYSELF. BUT I STILL CAN'T BELIEVE WE GOT THEM JUST FOR CLEANING UP OUR SCHOOL'S PLAYGROUND!

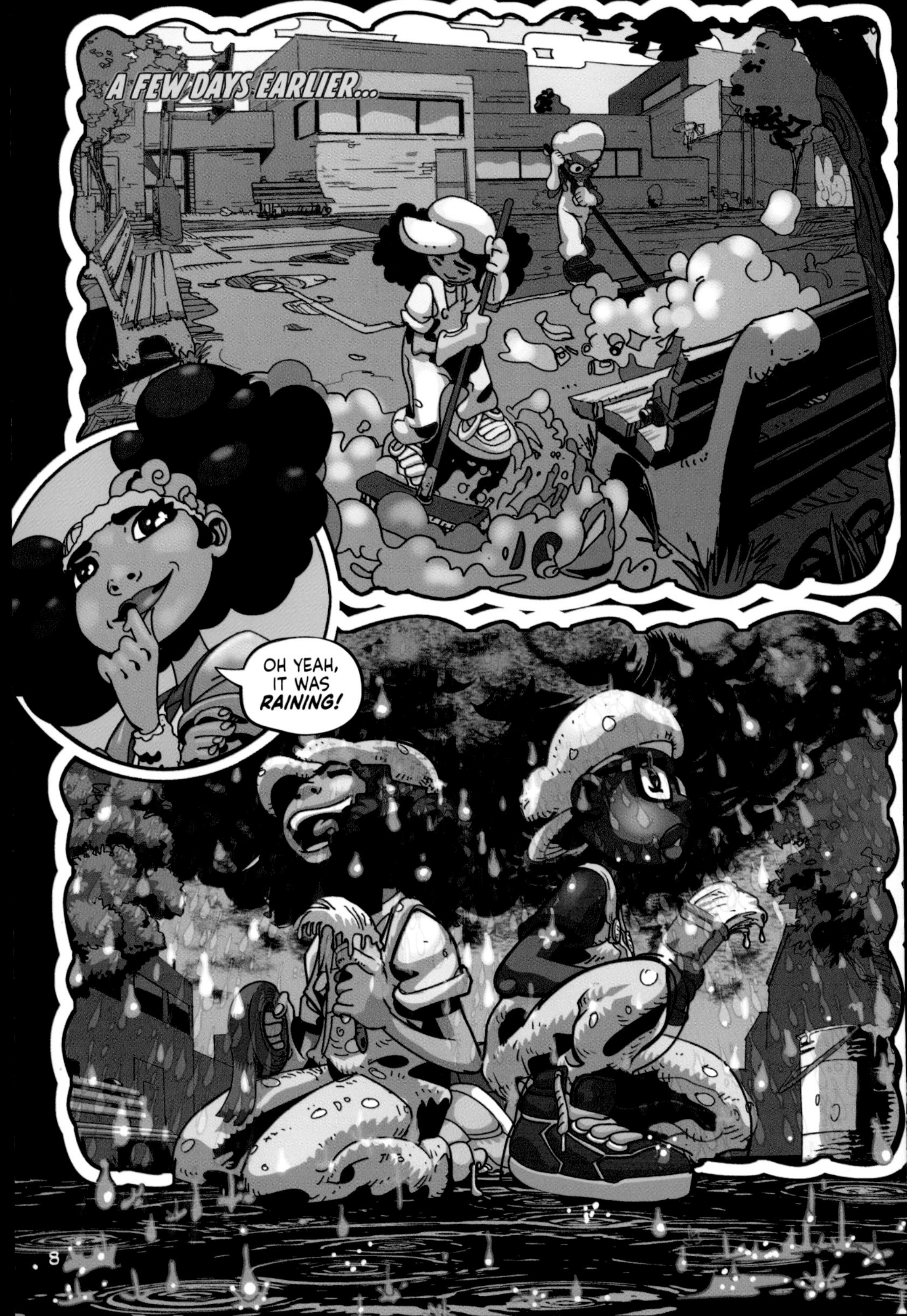
A FEW DAYS EARLIER...
OH YEAH, IT WAS RAINING!

ALLSTARS

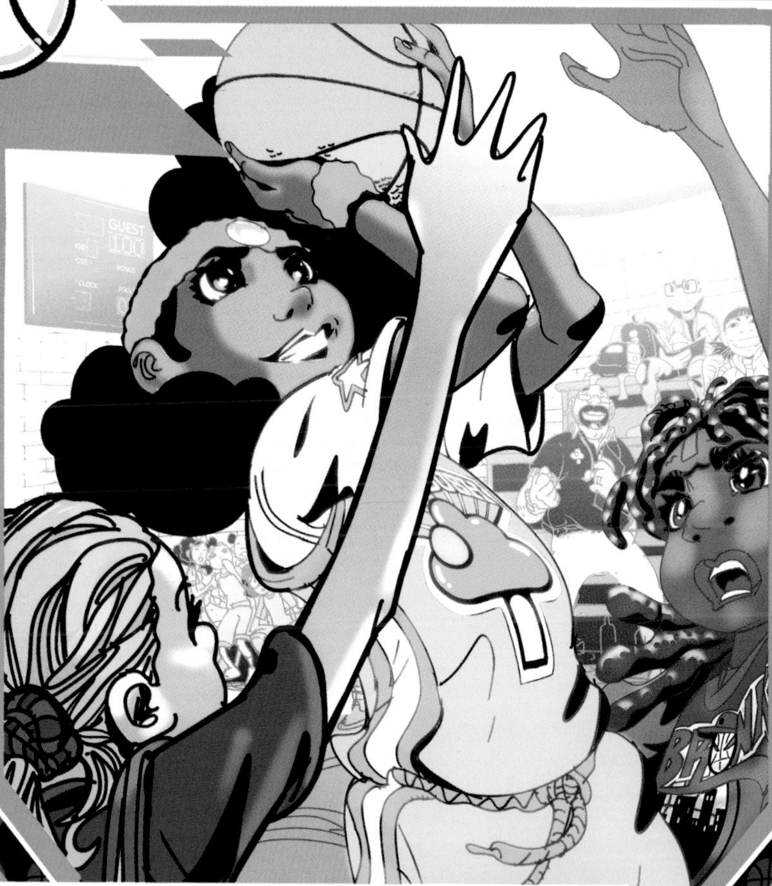

GUEST
100

MAYA MOSES

AGE: 11

- CAPTAIN OF HER SCHOOL'S BASKETBALL, SOCCER, BASEBALL, AND FLAG FOOTBALL TEAMS.
- FEARLESS, PASSIONATE, OUTSPOKEN, AND VERY CURIOUS. A *BIG* RISK-TAKER.

HEIGHT: 5'2"

- FAVORITE FOOD IS BUFFALO CHICKEN WINGS.
- FAVORITE PLAYER IS STEPHEN CURRY.

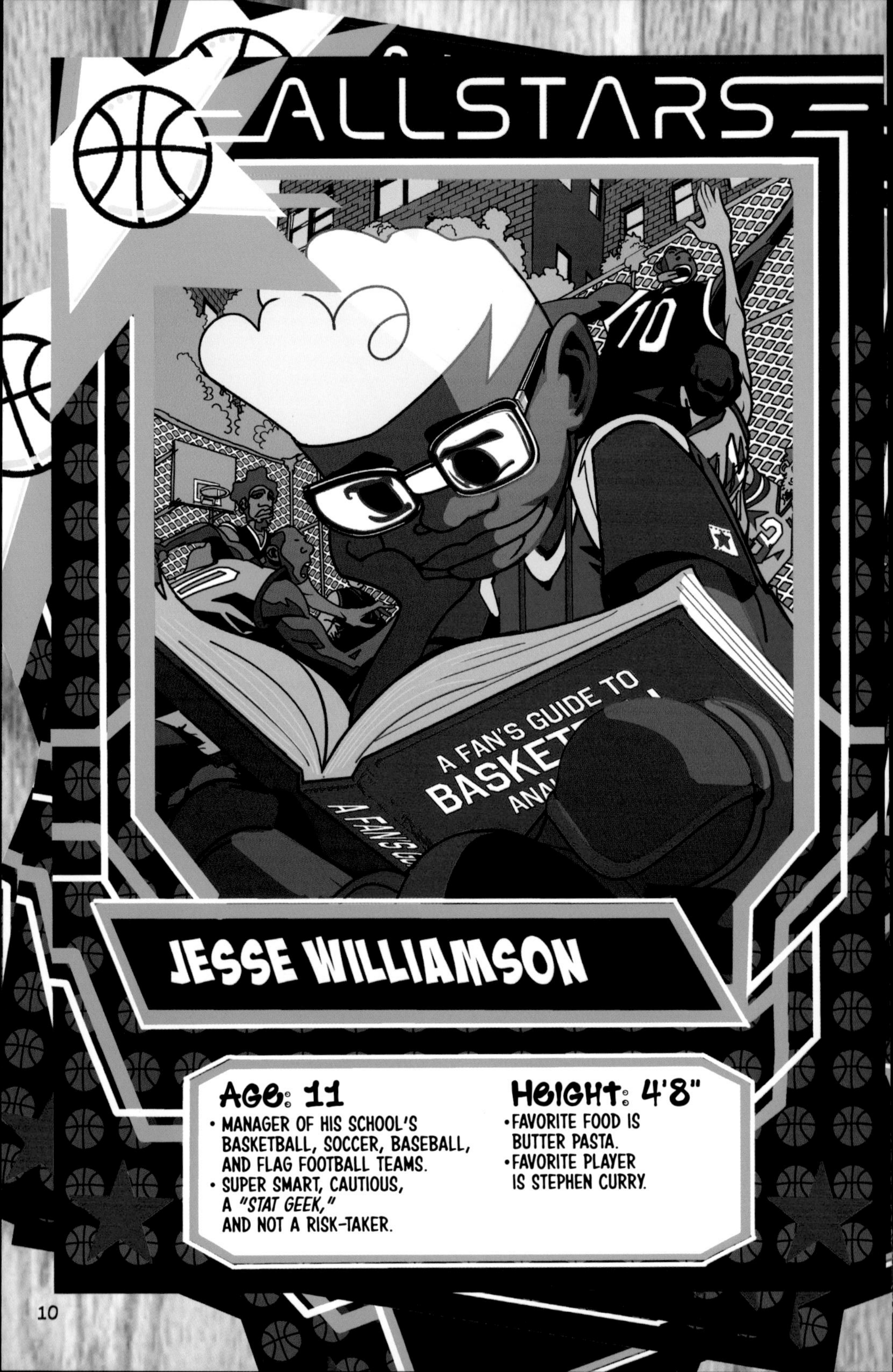
ALLSTARS
10
A FAN'S GUIDE TO BASKET
ANAL
JESSE WILLIAMSON
AGE: 11
• MANAGER OF HIS SCHOOL'S BASKETBALL, SOCCER, BASEBALL, AND FLAG FOOTBALL TEAMS.
• SUPER SMART, CAUTIOUS, A *"STAT GEEK,"* AND NOT A RISK-TAKER.
HEIGHT: 4'8"
•FAVORITE FOOD IS BUTTER PASTA.
•FAVORITE PLAYER IS STEPHEN CURRY.

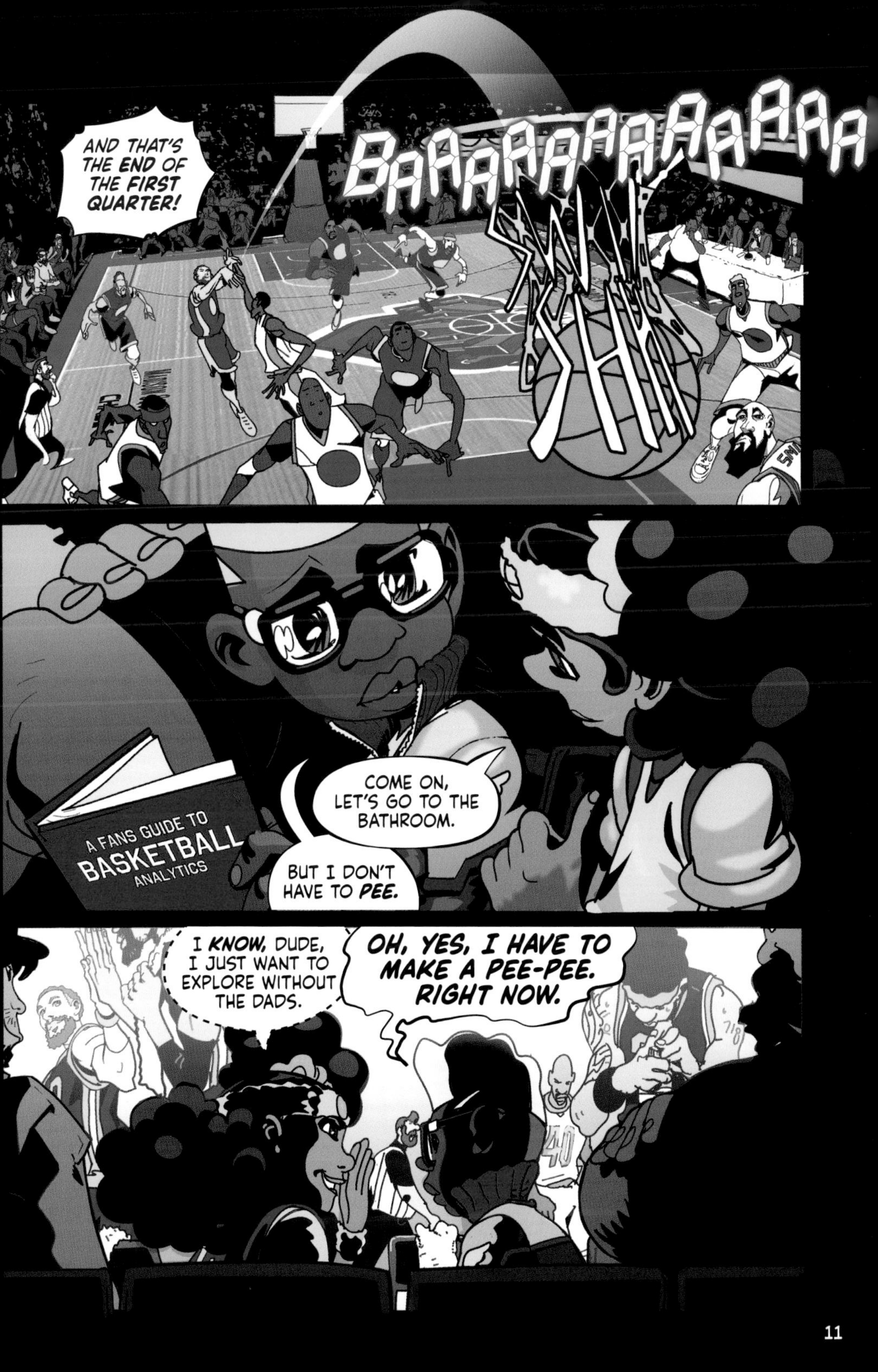
AND THAT'S THE END OF THE FIRST QUARTER!
BAAAAAAAAAAAAA
COME ON, LET'S GO TO THE BATHROOM.
BUT I DON'T HAVE TO PEE.
A FANS GUIDE TO BASKETBALL ANALYTICS
I KNOW, DUDE, I JUST WANT TO EXPLORE WITHOUT THE DADS.
OH, YES, I HAVE TO MAKE A PEE-PEE. RIGHT NOW.

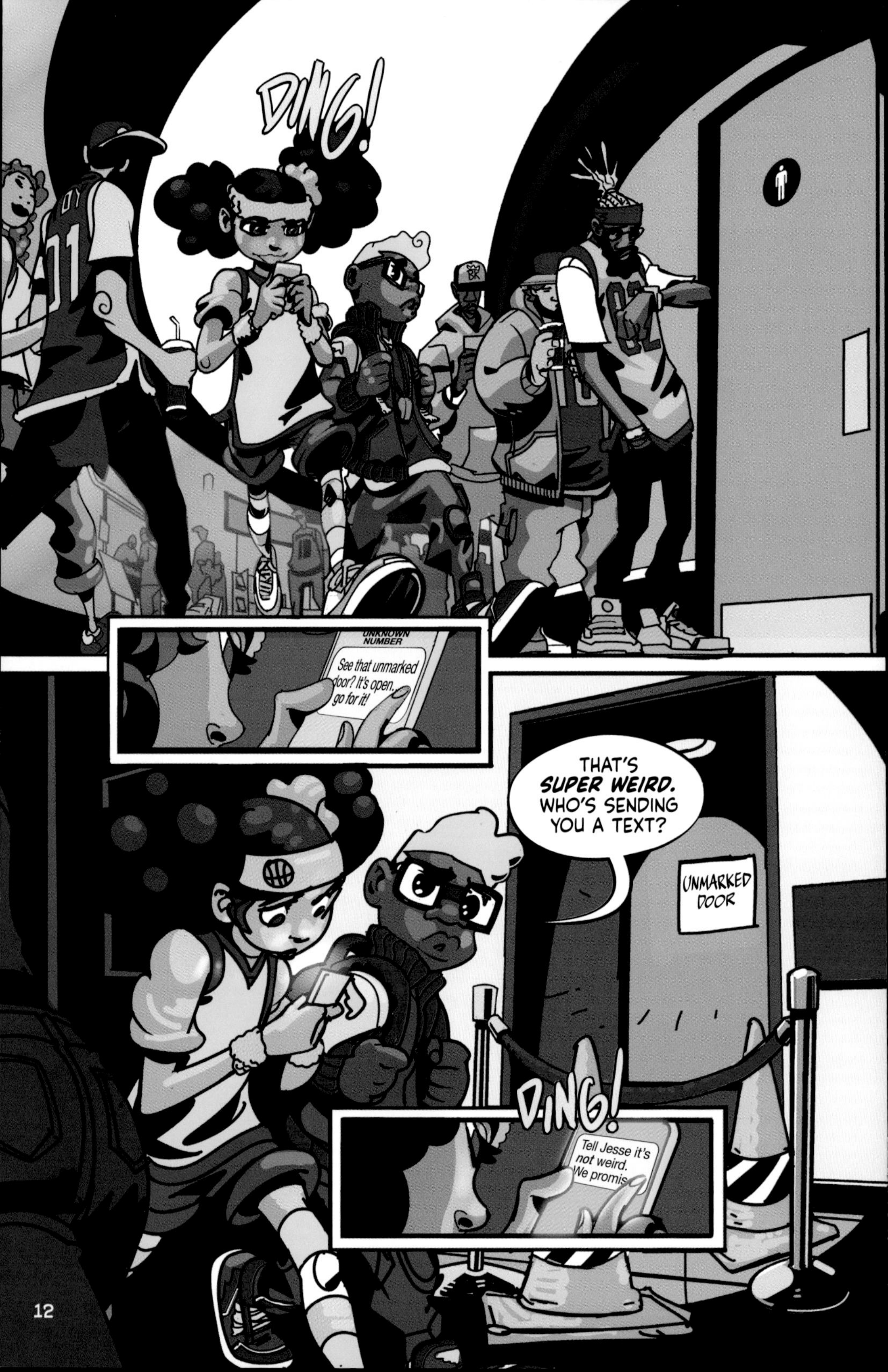
DING!
UNKNOWN NUMBER
See that unmarked door? It's open. go for it!
THAT'S *SUPER WEIRD.* WHO'S SENDING YOU A TEXT?
UNMARKED DOOR
DING!
Tell Jesse it's *not* weird. We promis

CHAPTER TWO

THIS IS WEIRD!

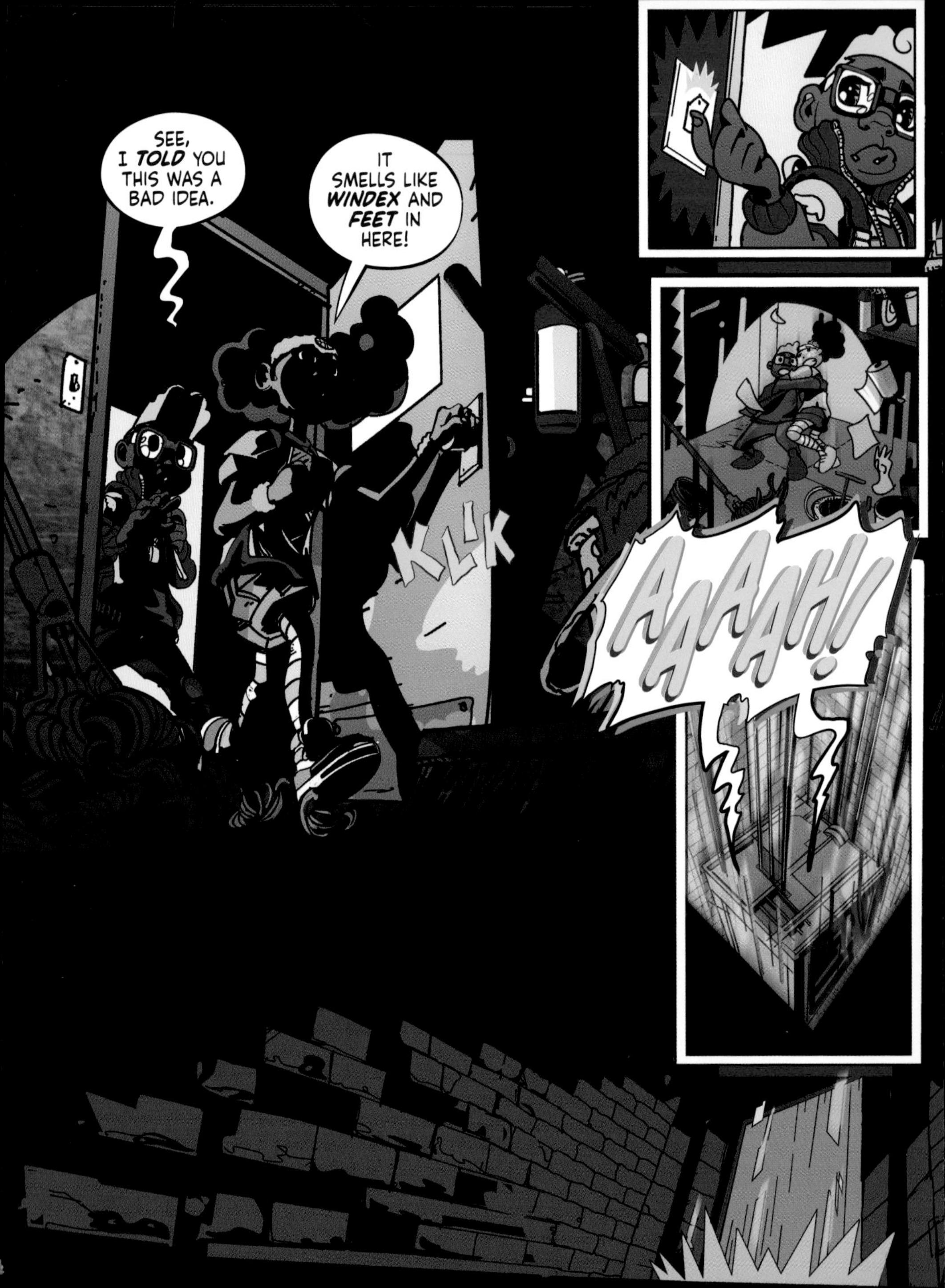
SEE, I TOLD YOU THIS WAS A BAD IDEA.
IT SMELLS LIKE WINDEX AND FEET IN HERE!
KLIK
AAAAAH!!

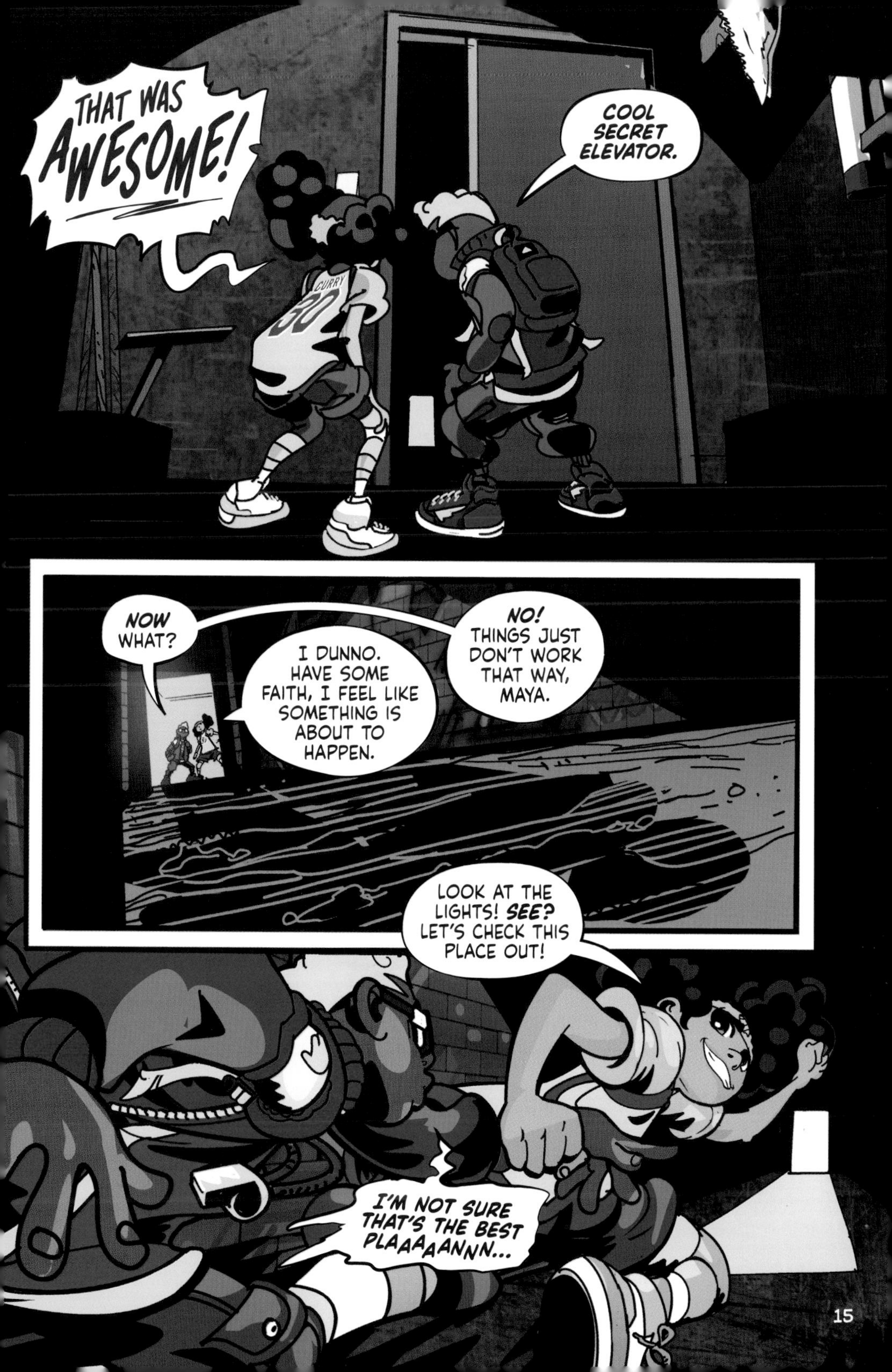
THAT WAS AWESOME!
COOL SECRET ELEVATOR.
CURRY 30
NOW WHAT?
I DUNNO. HAVE SOME FAITH, I FEEL LIKE SOMETHING IS ABOUT TO HAPPEN.
NO! THINGS JUST DON'T WORK THAT WAY, MAYA.
LOOK AT THE LIGHTS! SEE? LET'S CHECK THIS PLACE OUT!
I'M NOT SURE THAT'S THE BEST PLAAAAANNN...

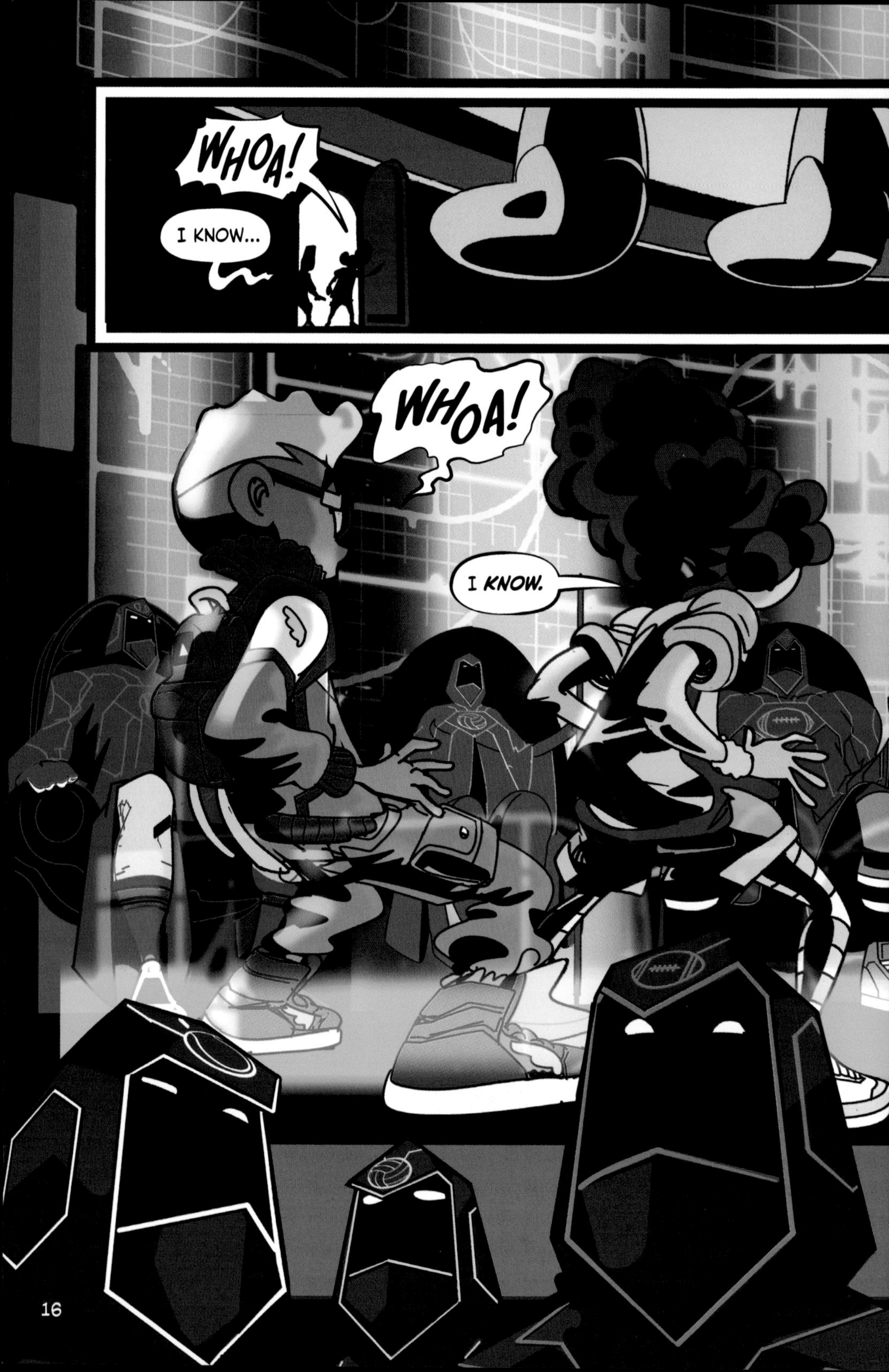
WHOA!
I KNOW...
WHOA!
I KNOW.

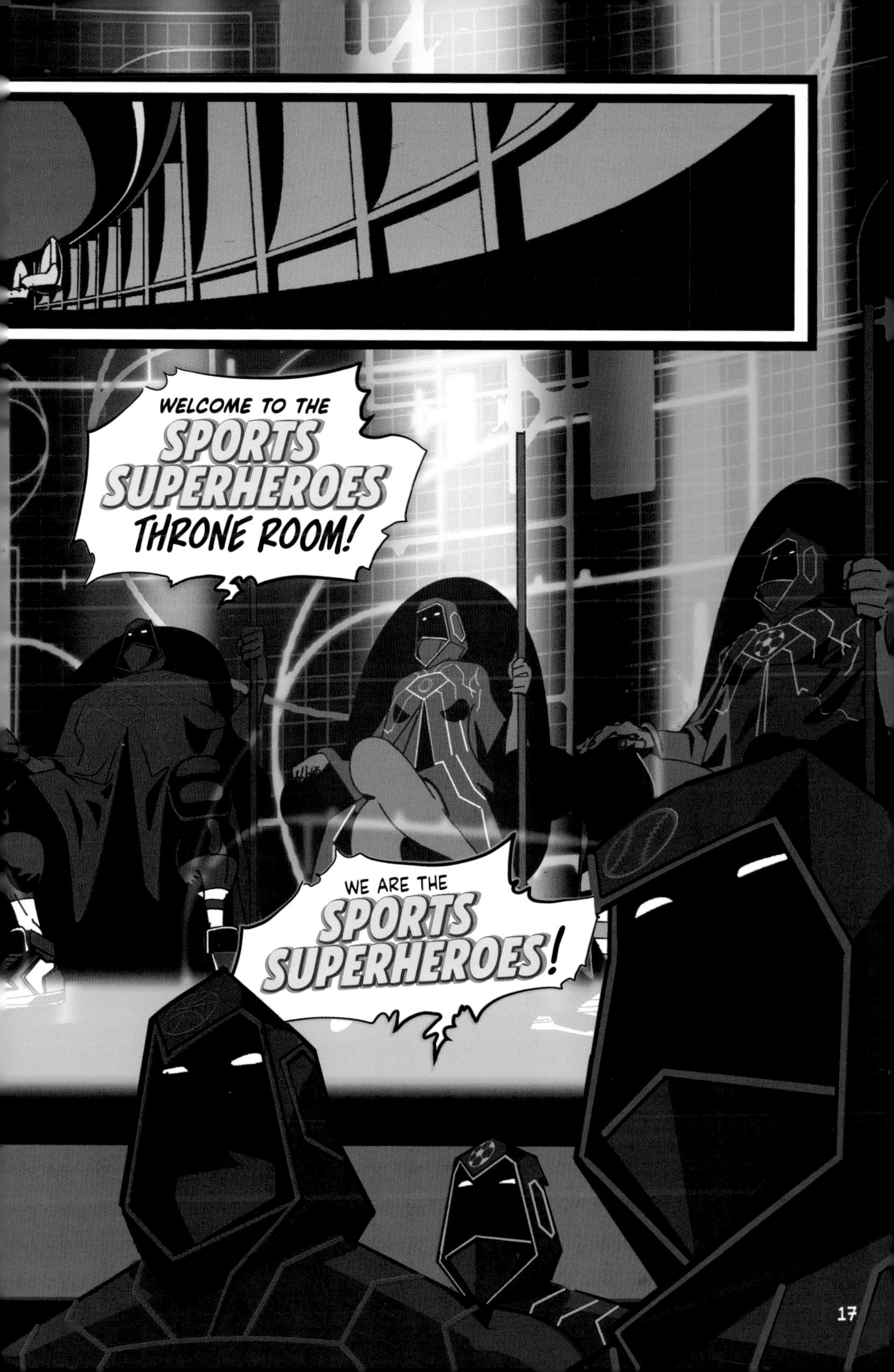
WELCOME TO THE SPORTS SUPERHEROES THRONE ROOM!
WE ARE THE SPORTS SUPERHEROES!

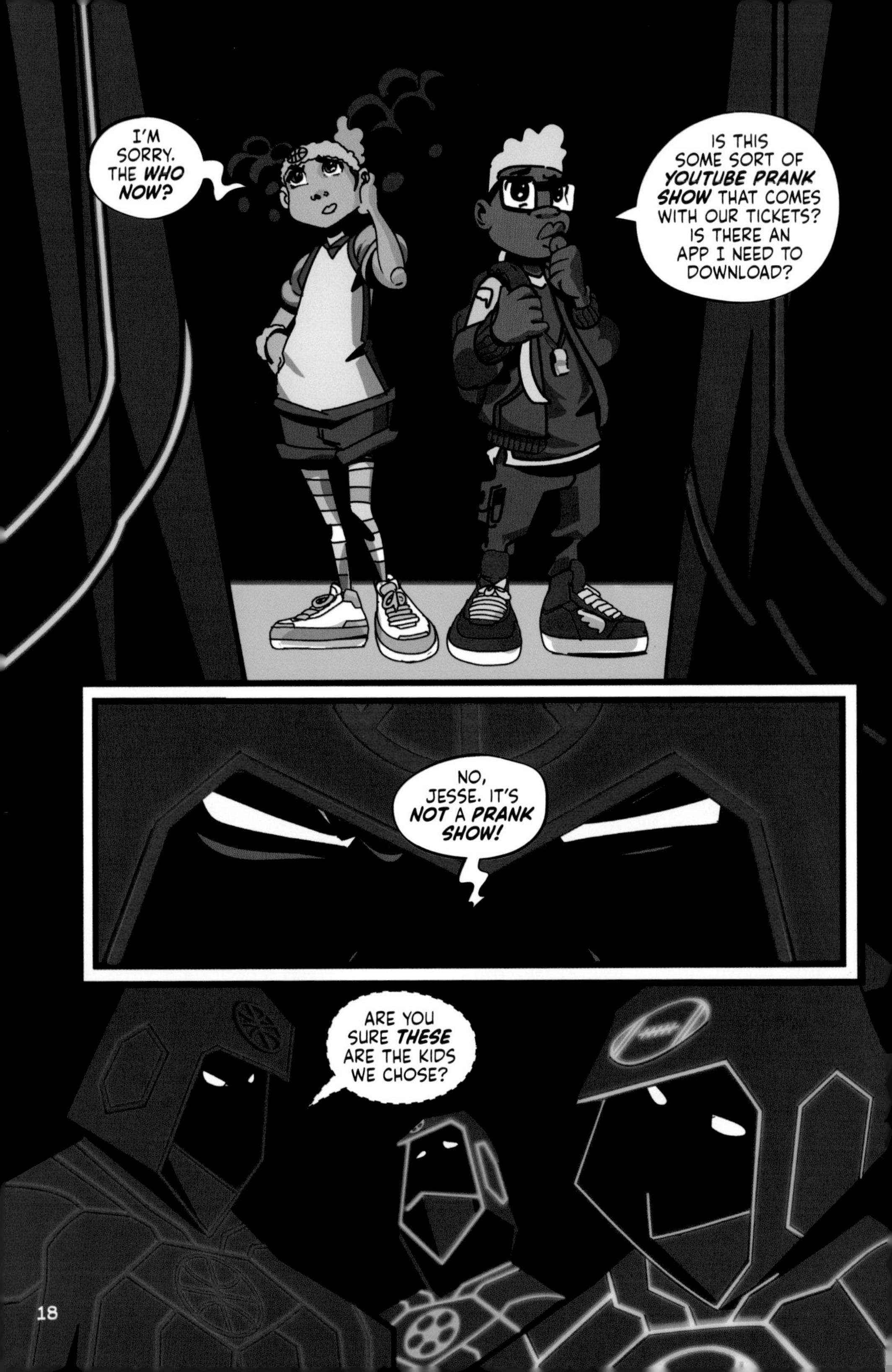
I'M SORRY. THE WHO NOW?
IS THIS SOME SORT OF YOUTUBE PRANK SHOW THAT COMES WITH OUR TICKETS? IS THERE AN APP I NEED TO DOWNLOAD?
NO, JESSE. IT'S NOT A PRANK SHOW!
ARE YOU SURE THESE ARE THE KIDS WE CHOSE?

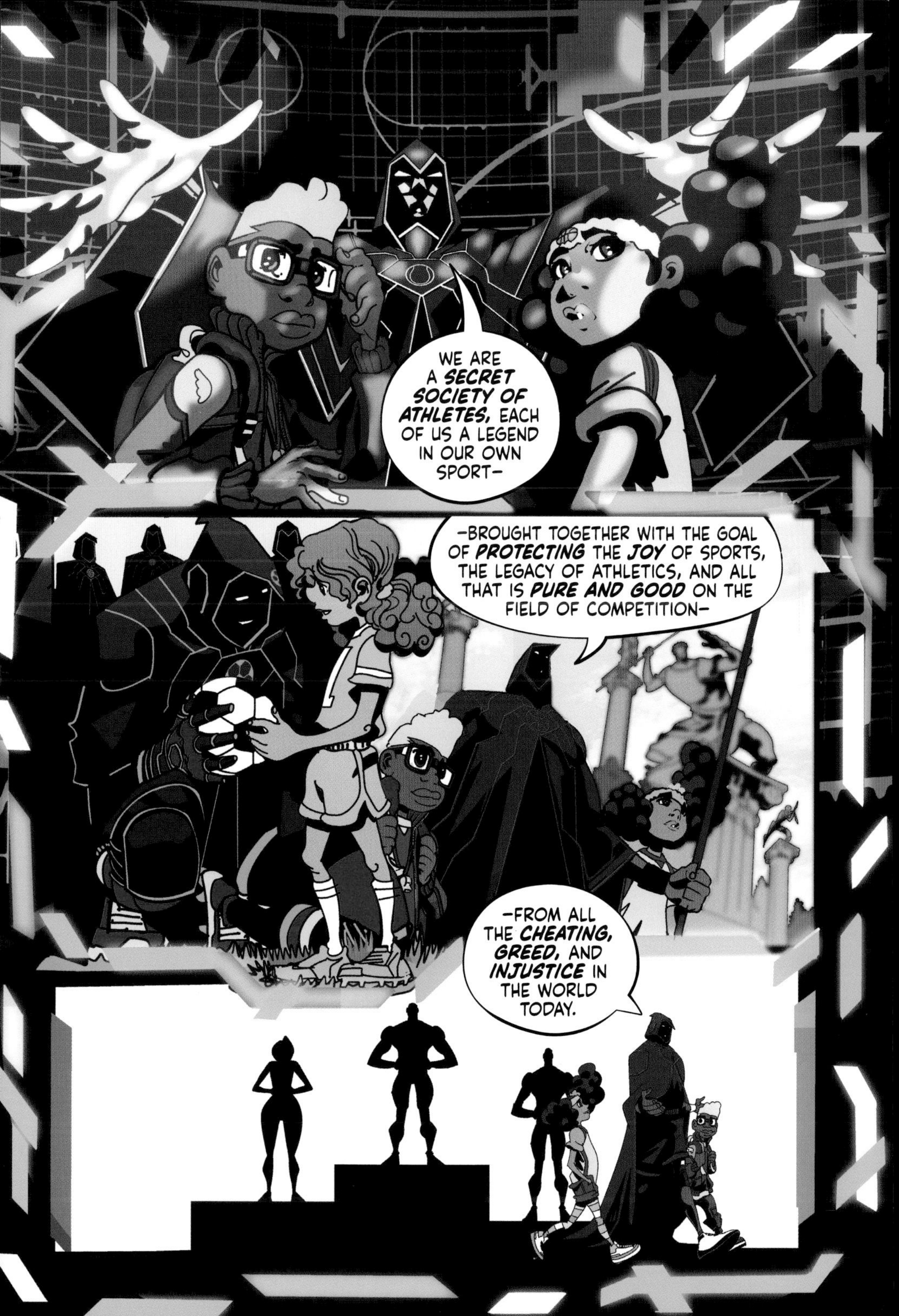
WE ARE A SECRET SOCIETY OF ATHLETES, EACH OF US A LEGEND IN OUR OWN SPORT–
–BROUGHT TOGETHER WITH THE GOAL OF PROTECTING THE JOY OF SPORTS, THE LEGACY OF ATHLETICS, AND ALL THAT IS PURE AND GOOD ON THE FIELD OF COMPETITION–
–FROM ALL THE CHEATING, GREED, AND INJUSTICE IN THE WORLD TODAY.

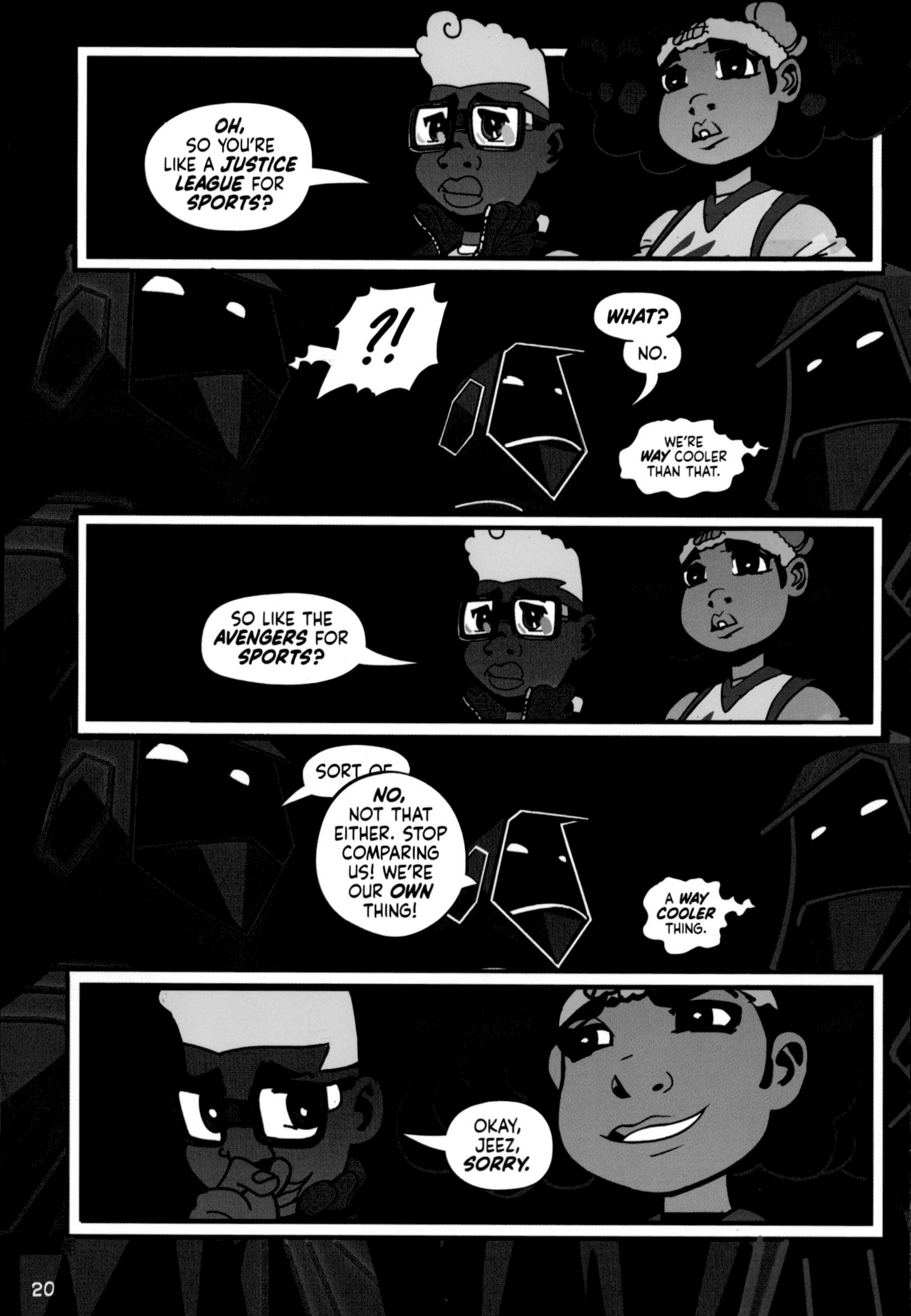
OH, SO YOU'RE LIKE A JUSTICE LEAGUE FOR SPORTS?
?!
WHAT?
NO.
WE'RE WAY COOLER THAN THAT.
SO LIKE THE AVENGERS FOR SPORTS?
SORT OF
NO, NOT THAT EITHER. STOP COMPARING US! WE'RE OUR OWN THING!
A WAY COOLER THING.
OKAY, JEEZ, SORRY.

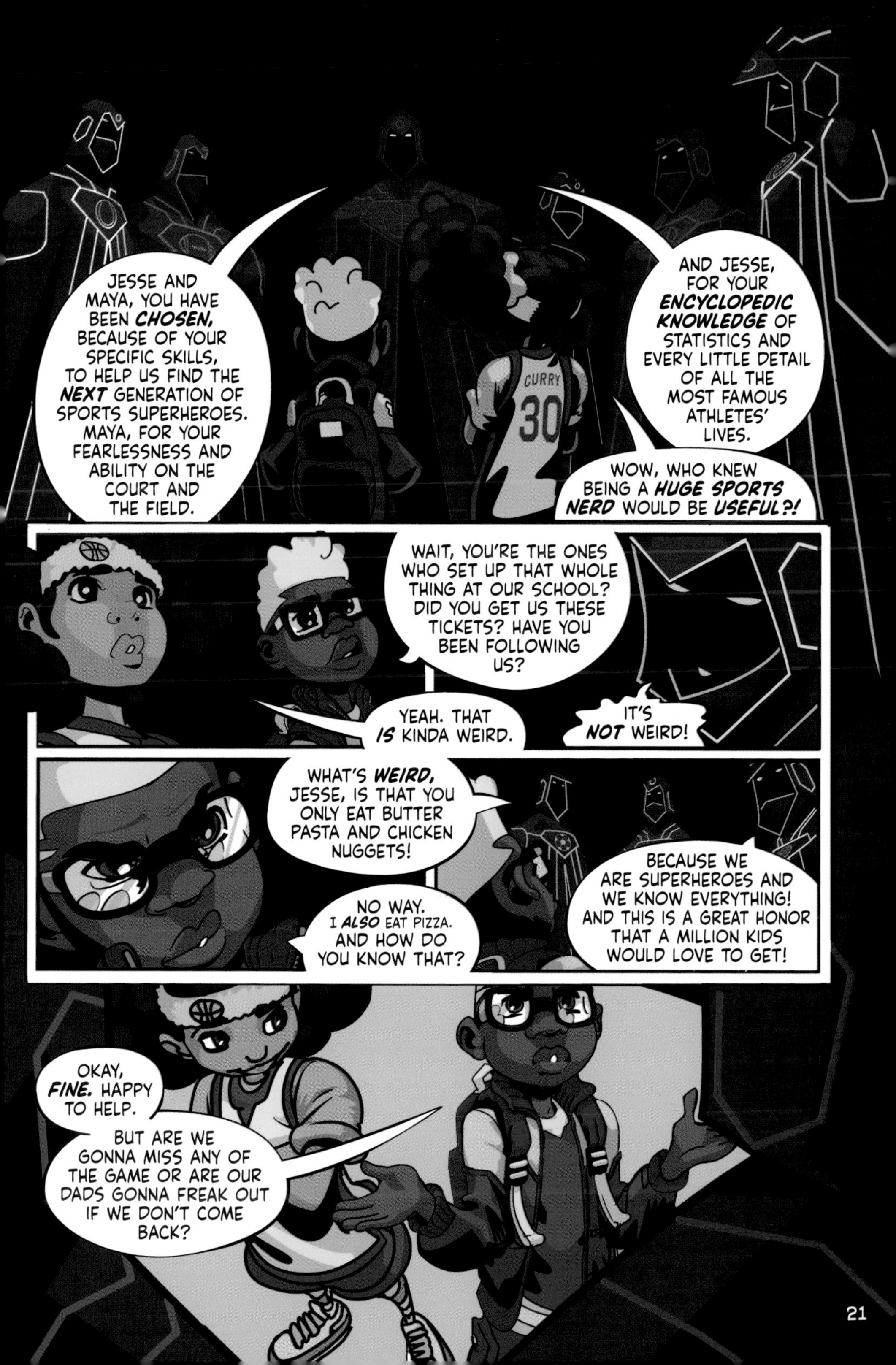
JESSE AND MAYA, YOU HAVE BEEN CHOSEN, BECAUSE OF YOUR SPECIFIC SKILLS, TO HELP US FIND THE NEXT GENERATION OF SPORTS SUPERHEROES. MAYA, FOR YOUR FEARLESSNESS AND ABILITY ON THE COURT AND THE FIELD.
CURRY 30
AND JESSE, FOR YOUR ENCYCLOPEDIC KNOWLEDGE OF STATISTICS AND EVERY LITTLE DETAIL OF ALL THE MOST FAMOUS ATHLETES' LIVES.
WOW, WHO KNEW BEING A HUGE SPORTS NERD WOULD BE USEFUL?!
WAIT, YOU'RE THE ONES WHO SET UP THAT WHOLE THING AT OUR SCHOOL? DID YOU GET US THESE TICKETS? HAVE YOU BEEN FOLLOWING US?
YEAH. THAT IS KINDA WEIRD.
IT'S NOT WEIRD!
WHAT'S WEIRD, JESSE, IS THAT YOU ONLY EAT BUTTER PASTA AND CHICKEN NUGGETS!
NO WAY. I ALSO EAT PIZZA. AND HOW DO YOU KNOW THAT?
BECAUSE WE ARE SUPERHEROES AND WE KNOW EVERYTHING! AND THIS IS A GREAT HONOR THAT A MILLION KIDS WOULD LOVE TO GET!
OKAY, FINE. HAPPY TO HELP.
BUT ARE WE GONNA MISS ANY OF THE GAME OR ARE OUR DADS GONNA FREAK OUT IF WE DON'T COME BACK?

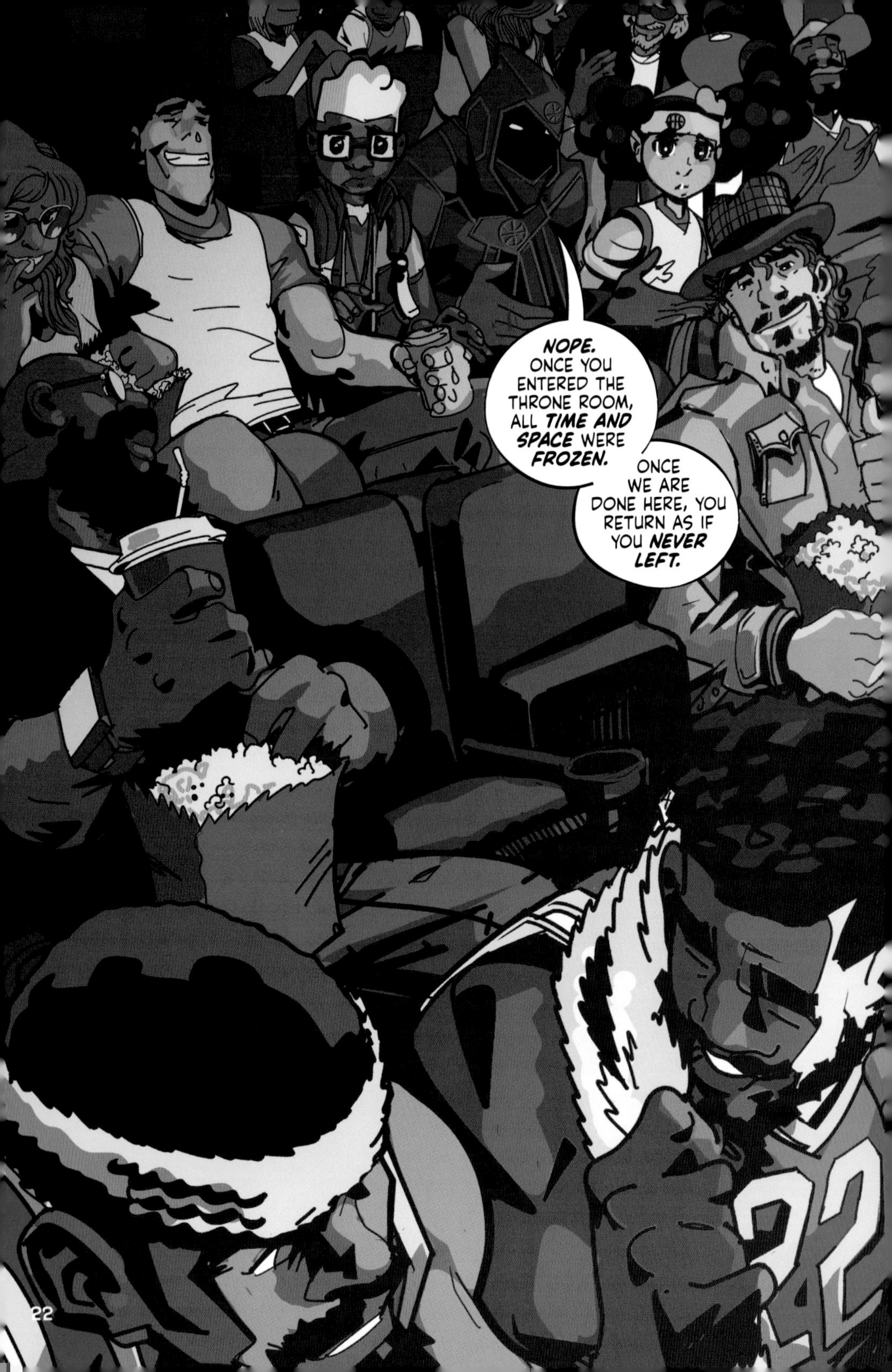
NOPE. ONCE YOU ENTERED THE THRONE ROOM, ALL TIME AND SPACE WERE FROZEN.
ONCE WE ARE DONE HERE, YOU RETURN AS IF YOU NEVER LEFT.

CHAPTER THREE

THE NEXT GENERATION

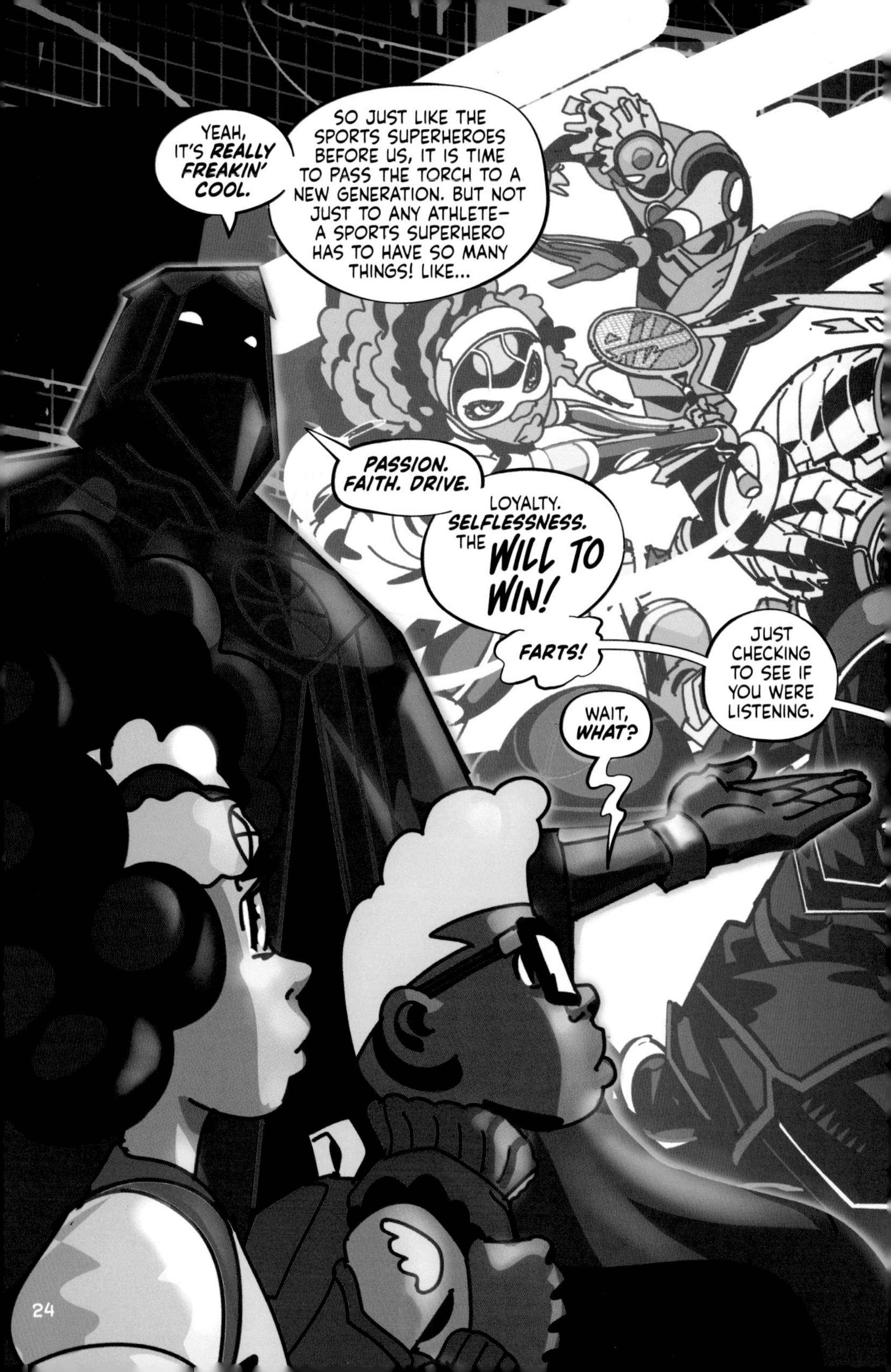
YEAH, IT'S REALLY FREAKIN' COOL.
SO JUST LIKE THE SPORTS SUPERHEROES BEFORE US, IT IS TIME TO PASS THE TORCH TO A NEW GENERATION. BUT NOT JUST TO ANY ATHLETE— A SPORTS SUPERHERO HAS TO HAVE SO MANY THINGS! LIKE...
PASSION. FAITH. DRIVE.
LOYALTY. SELFLESSNESS. THE WILL TO WIN!
FARTS!
JUST CHECKING TO SEE IF YOU WERE LISTENING.
WAIT, WHAT?

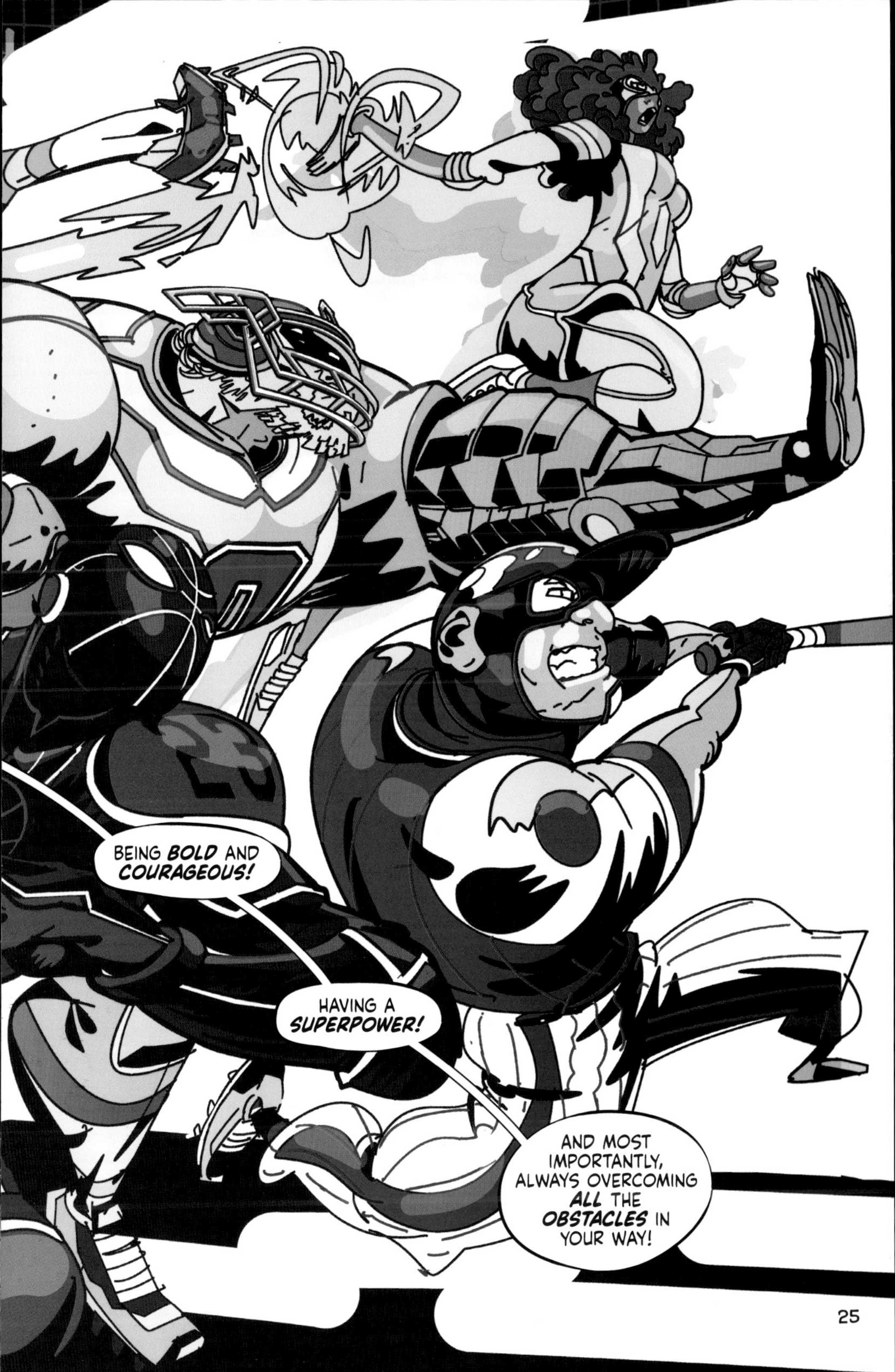
BEING **BOLD** AND **COURAGEOUS!**
HAVING A **SUPERPOWER!**
AND MOST IMPORTANTLY, ALWAYS OVERCOMING **ALL** THE **OBSTACLES** IN YOUR WAY!

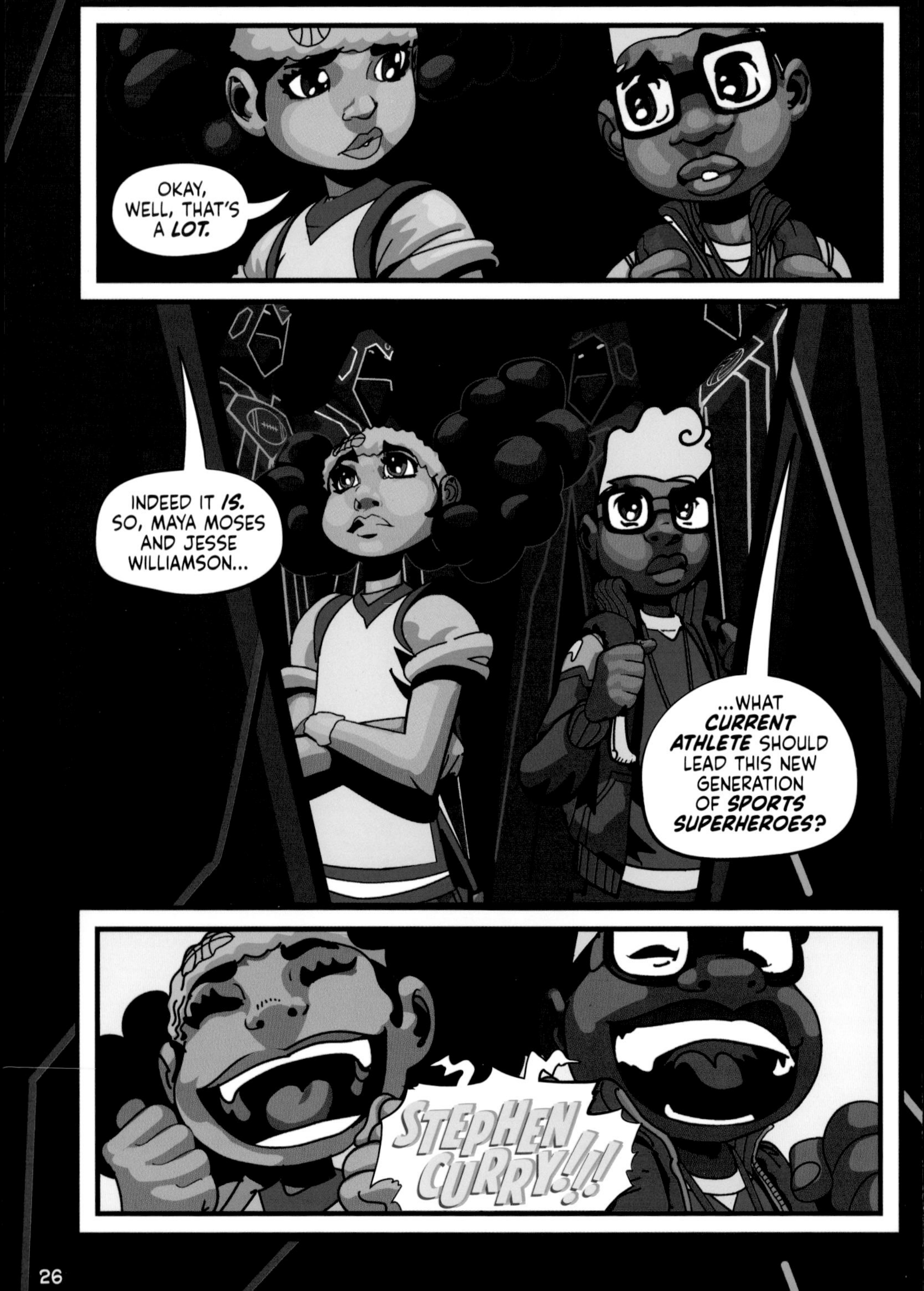
OKAY, WELL, THAT'S A *LOT.*
INDEED IT *IS.* SO, MAYA MOSES AND JESSE WILLIAMSON...
...WHAT *CURRENT ATHLETE* SHOULD LEAD THIS NEW GENERATION OF *SPORTS SUPERHEROES?*
STEPHEN CURRY!!!

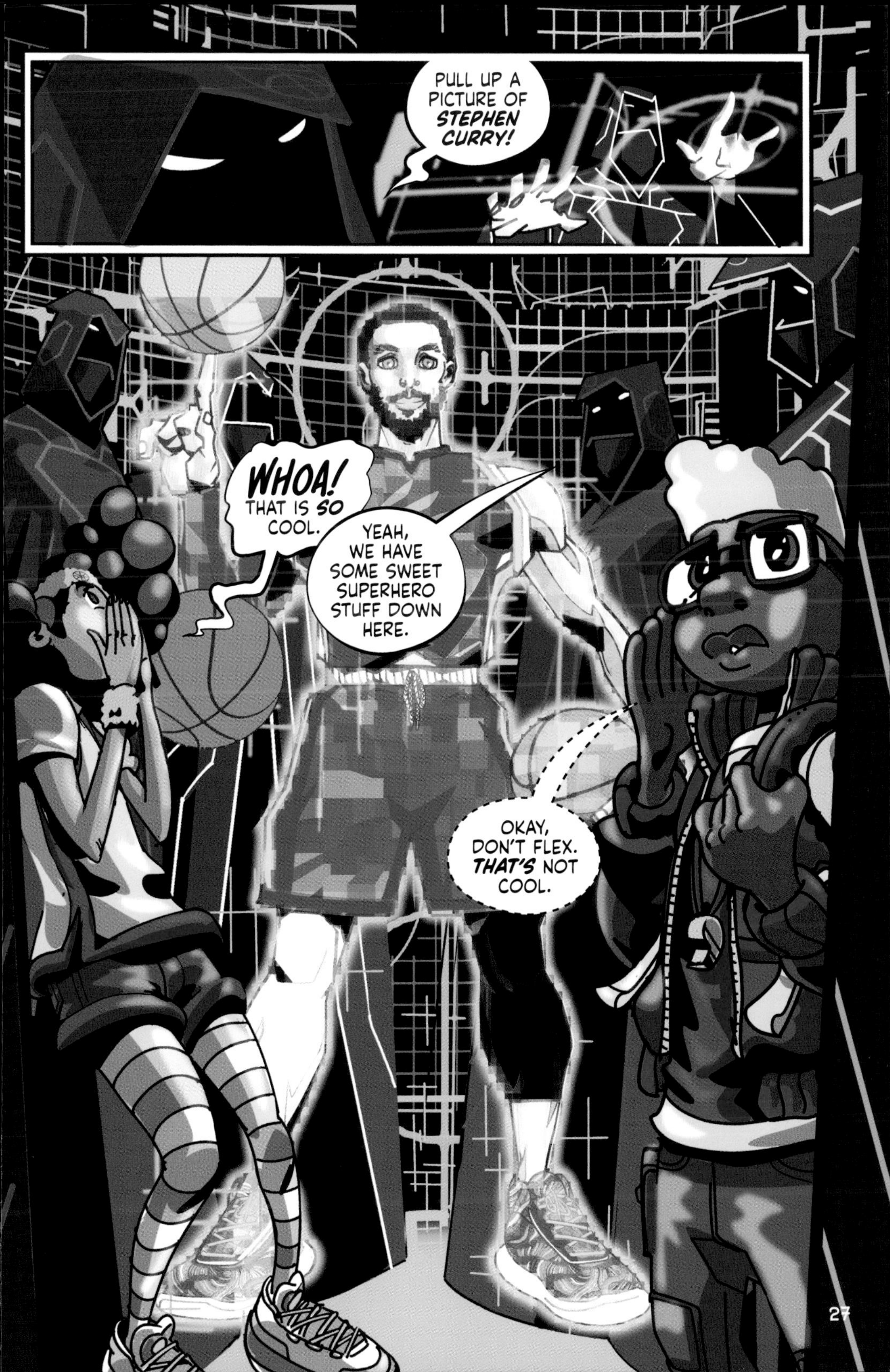
PULL UP A PICTURE OF STEPHEN CURRY!
WHOA! THAT IS SO COOL.
YEAH, WE HAVE SOME SWEET SUPERHERO STUFF DOWN HERE.
OKAY, DON'T FLEX. THAT'S NOT COOL.

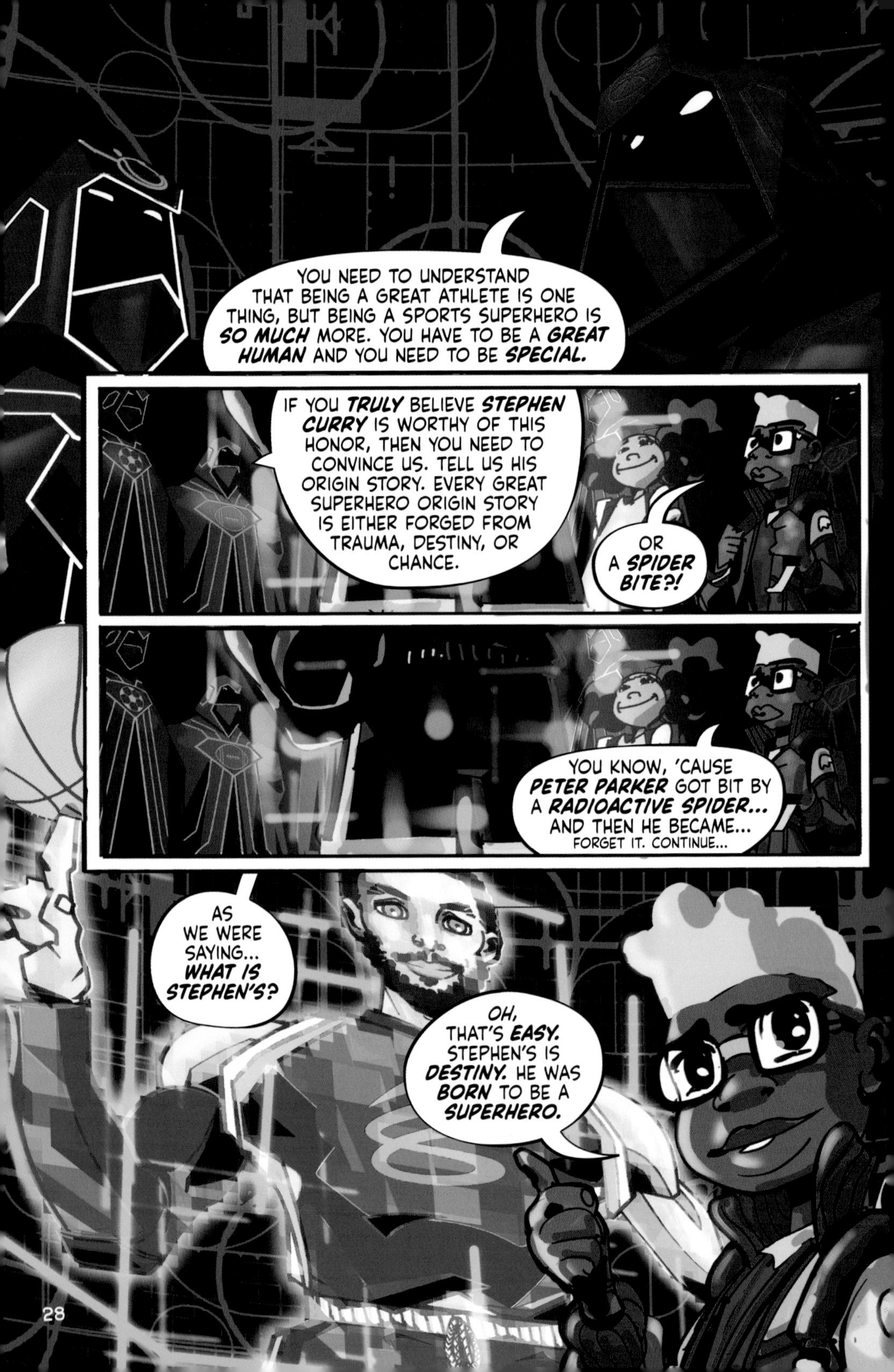
YOU NEED TO UNDERSTAND THAT BEING A GREAT ATHLETE IS ONE THING, BUT BEING A SPORTS SUPERHERO IS ***SO MUCH*** MORE. YOU HAVE TO BE A ***GREAT HUMAN*** AND YOU NEED TO BE ***SPECIAL.***
IF YOU ***TRULY*** BELIEVE ***STEPHEN CURRY*** IS WORTHY OF THIS HONOR, THEN YOU NEED TO CONVINCE US. TELL US HIS ORIGIN STORY. EVERY GREAT SUPERHERO ORIGIN STORY IS EITHER FORGED FROM TRAUMA, DESTINY, OR CHANCE.
OR A ***SPIDER BITE?!***
YOU KNOW, 'CAUSE ***PETER PARKER*** GOT BIT BY A ***RADIOACTIVE SPIDER...*** AND THEN HE BECAME... FORGET IT. CONTINUE...
AS WE WERE SAYING... ***WHAT IS STEPHEN'S?***
OH, THAT'S ***EASY.*** STEPHEN'S IS ***DESTINY.*** HE WAS ***BORN*** TO BE A ***SUPERHERO.***

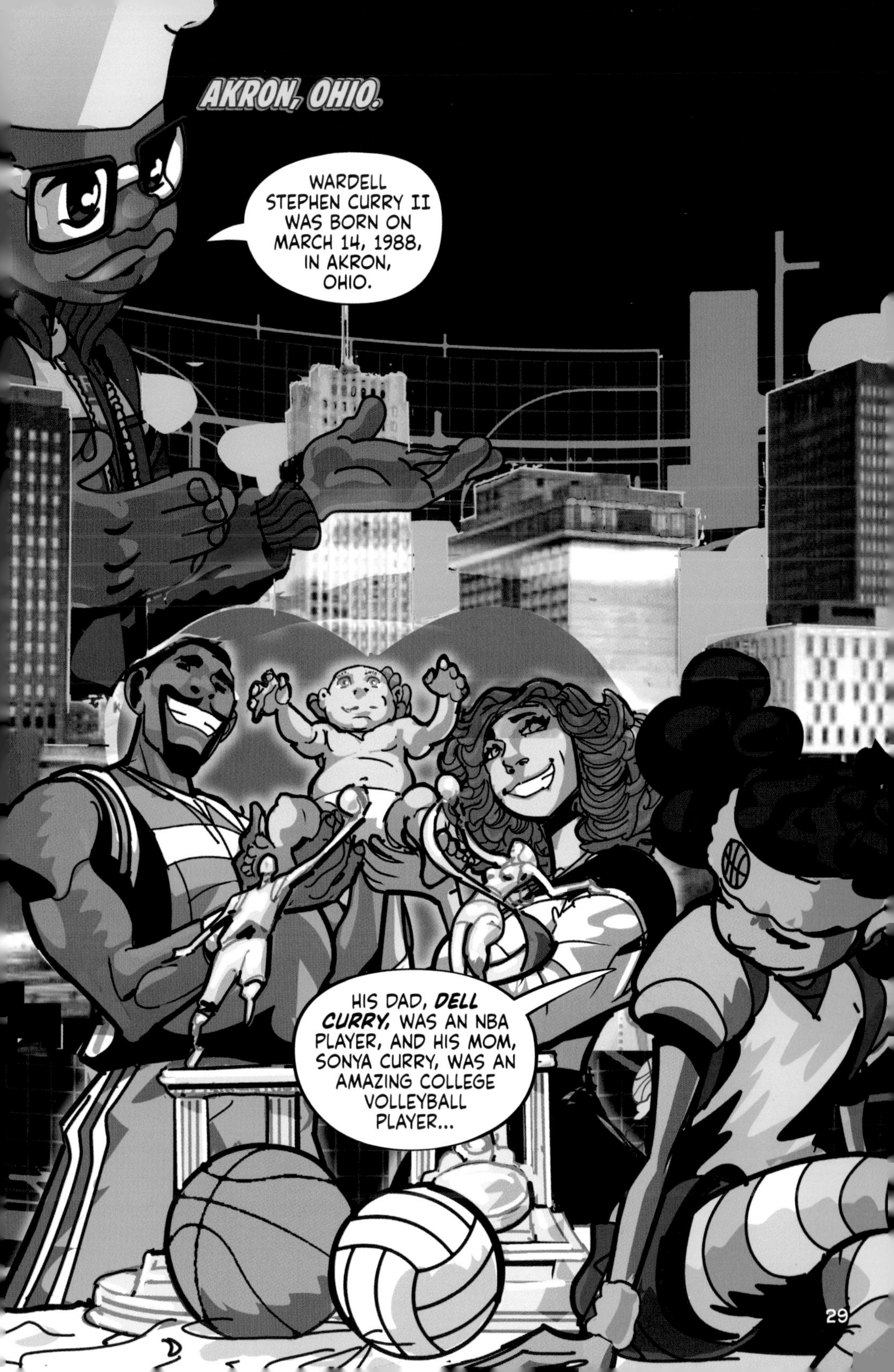
AKRON, OHIO.
WARDELL STEPHEN CURRY II WAS BORN ON MARCH 14, 1988, IN AKRON, OHIO.
HIS DAD, **DELL CURRY,** WAS AN NBA PLAYER, AND HIS MOM, SONYA CURRY, WAS AN AMAZING COLLEGE VOLLEYBALL PLAYER...

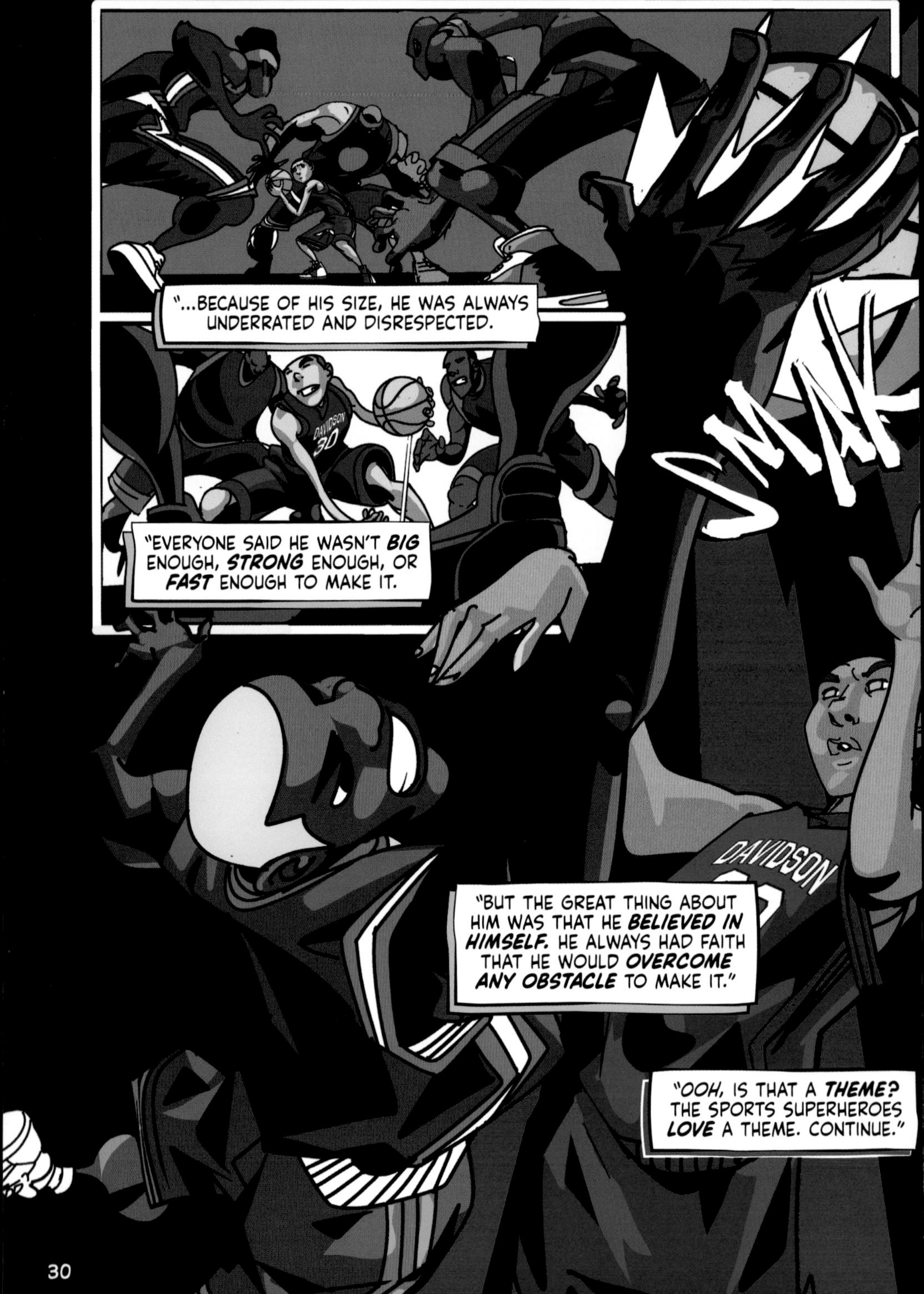
"...BECAUSE OF HIS SIZE, HE WAS ALWAYS UNDERRATED AND DISRESPECTED.
"EVERYONE SAID HE WASN'T **BIG** ENOUGH, **STRONG** ENOUGH, OR **FAST** ENOUGH TO MAKE IT.
SMAK
DAVIDSON
"BUT THE GREAT THING ABOUT HIM WAS THAT HE **BELIEVED IN HIMSELF.** HE ALWAYS HAD FAITH THAT HE WOULD **OVERCOME ANY OBSTACLE** TO MAKE IT."
"OOH, IS THAT A **THEME?** THE SPORTS SUPERHEROES **LOVE** A THEME. CONTINUE."

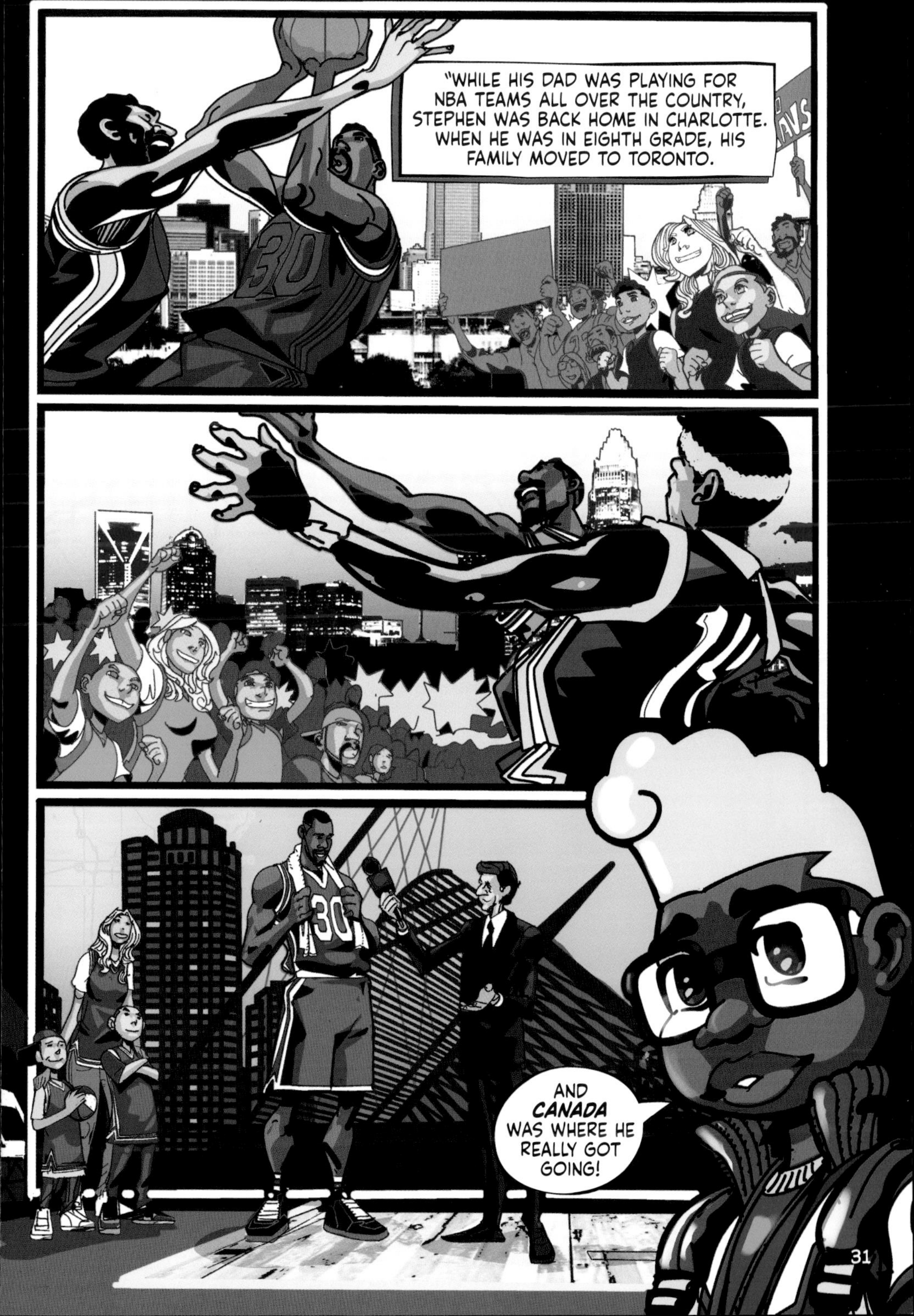
"WHILE HIS DAD WAS PLAYING FOR NBA TEAMS ALL OVER THE COUNTRY, STEPHEN WAS BACK HOME IN CHARLOTTE. WHEN HE WAS IN EIGHTH GRADE, HIS FAMILY MOVED TO TORONTO.
AND *CANADA* WAS WHERE HE REALLY GOT GOING!

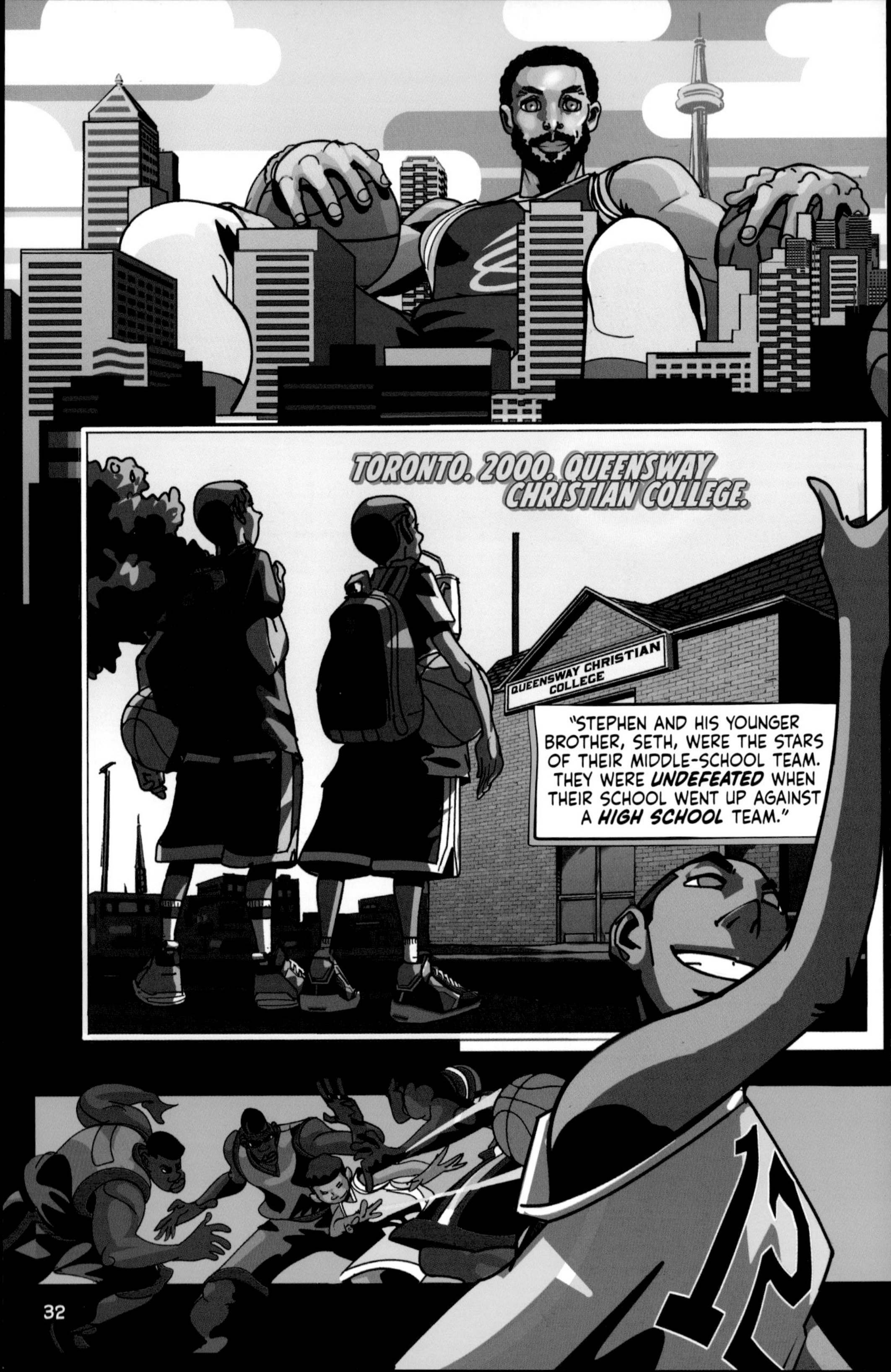
TORONTO. 2000. QUEENSWAY CHRISTIAN COLLEGE.
QUEENSWAY CHRISTIAN COLLEGE
"STEPHEN AND HIS YOUNGER BROTHER, SETH, WERE THE STARS OF THEIR MIDDLE-SCHOOL TEAM. THEY WERE *UNDEFEATED* WHEN THEIR SCHOOL WENT UP AGAINST A *HIGH SCHOOL* TEAM."

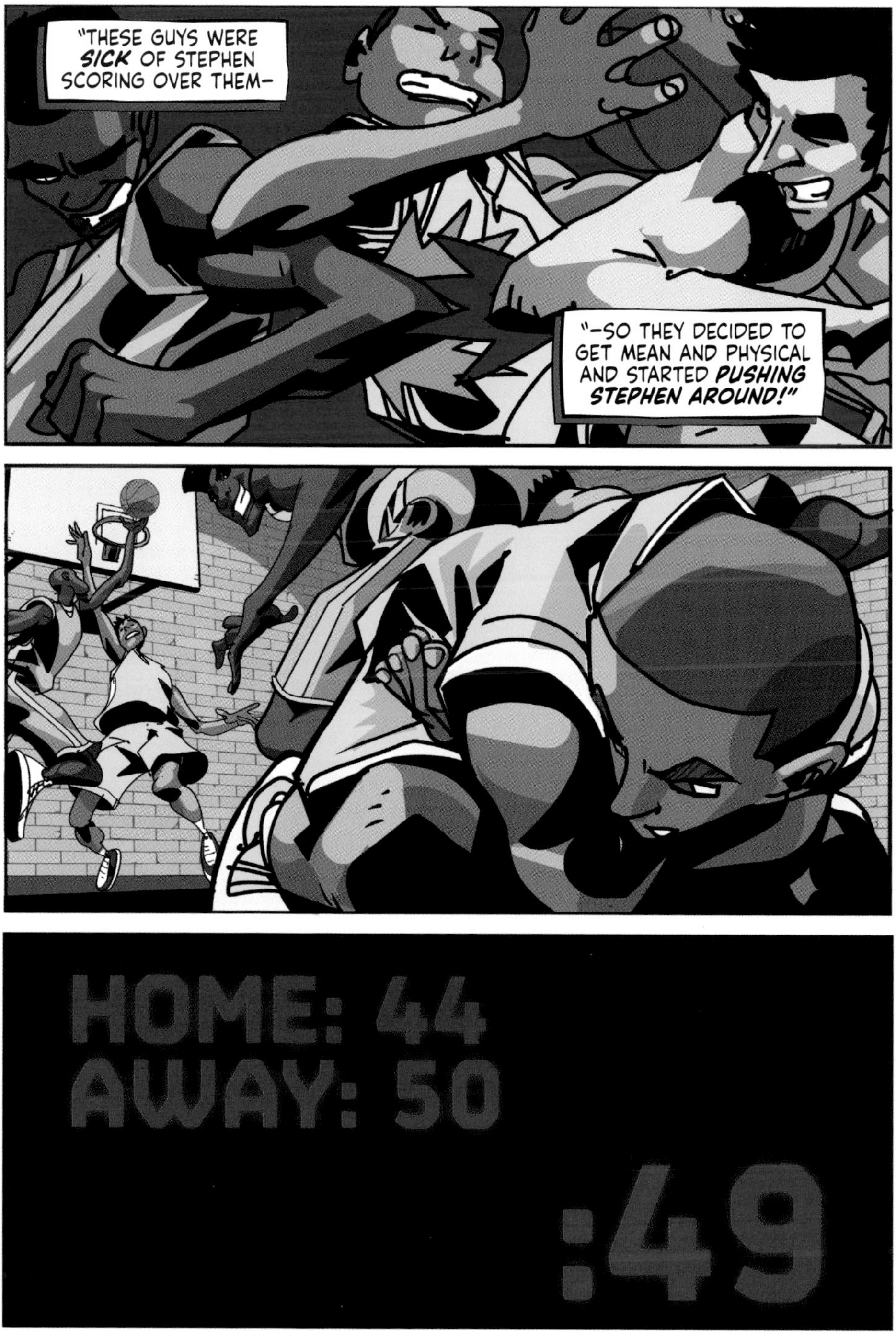
"THESE GUYS WERE SICK OF STEPHEN SCORING OVER THEM–
"–SO THEY DECIDED TO GET MEAN AND PHYSICAL AND STARTED PUSHING STEPHEN AROUND!"
HOME: 44
AWAY: 50
:49

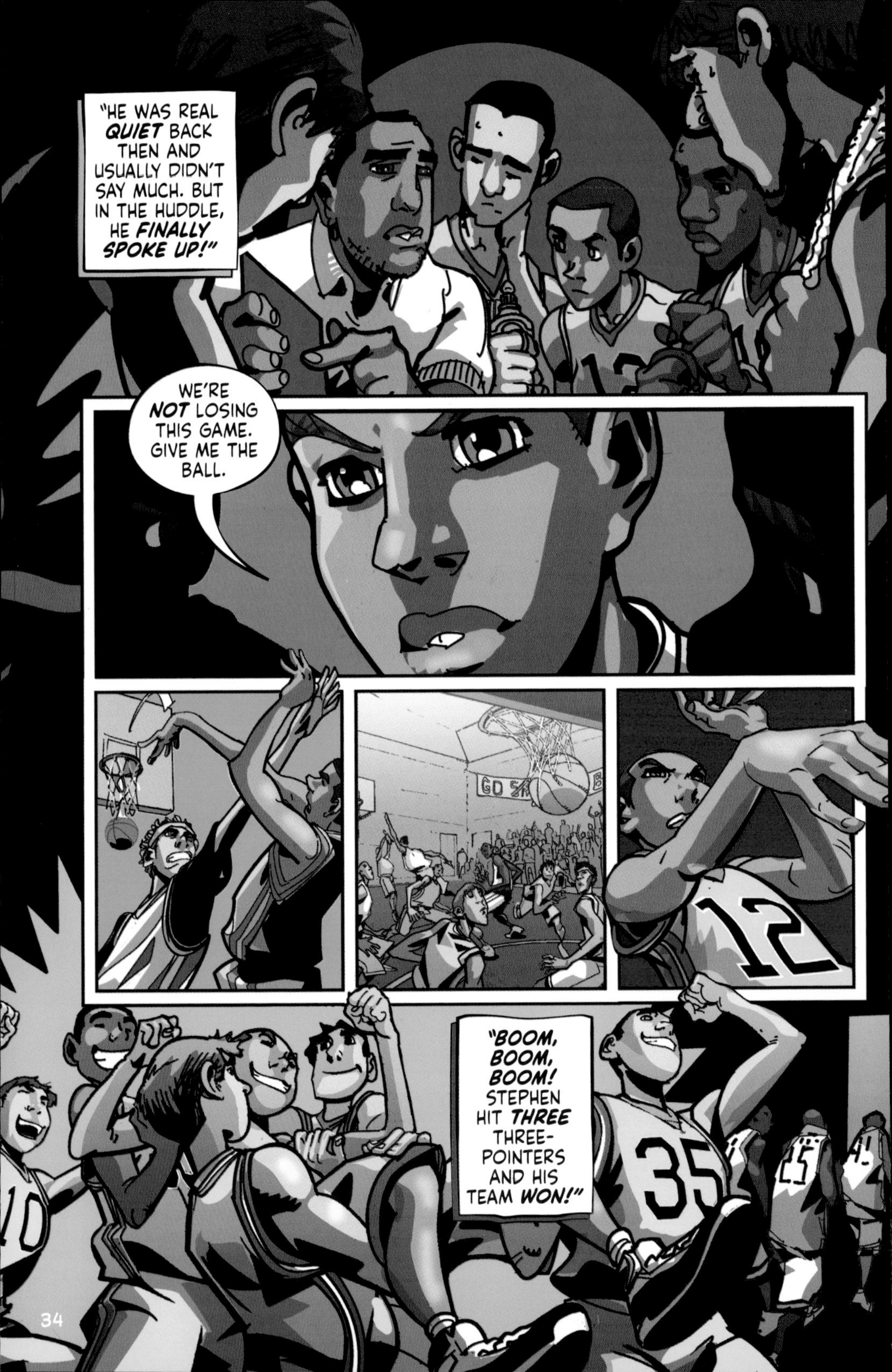
"HE WAS REAL QUIET BACK THEN AND USUALLY DIDN'T SAY MUCH. BUT IN THE HUDDLE, HE FINALLY SPOKE UP!"
WE'RE NOT LOSING THIS GAME. GIVE ME THE BALL.
"BOOM, BOOM, BOOM! STEPHEN HIT THREE THREE-POINTERS AND HIS TEAM WON!"

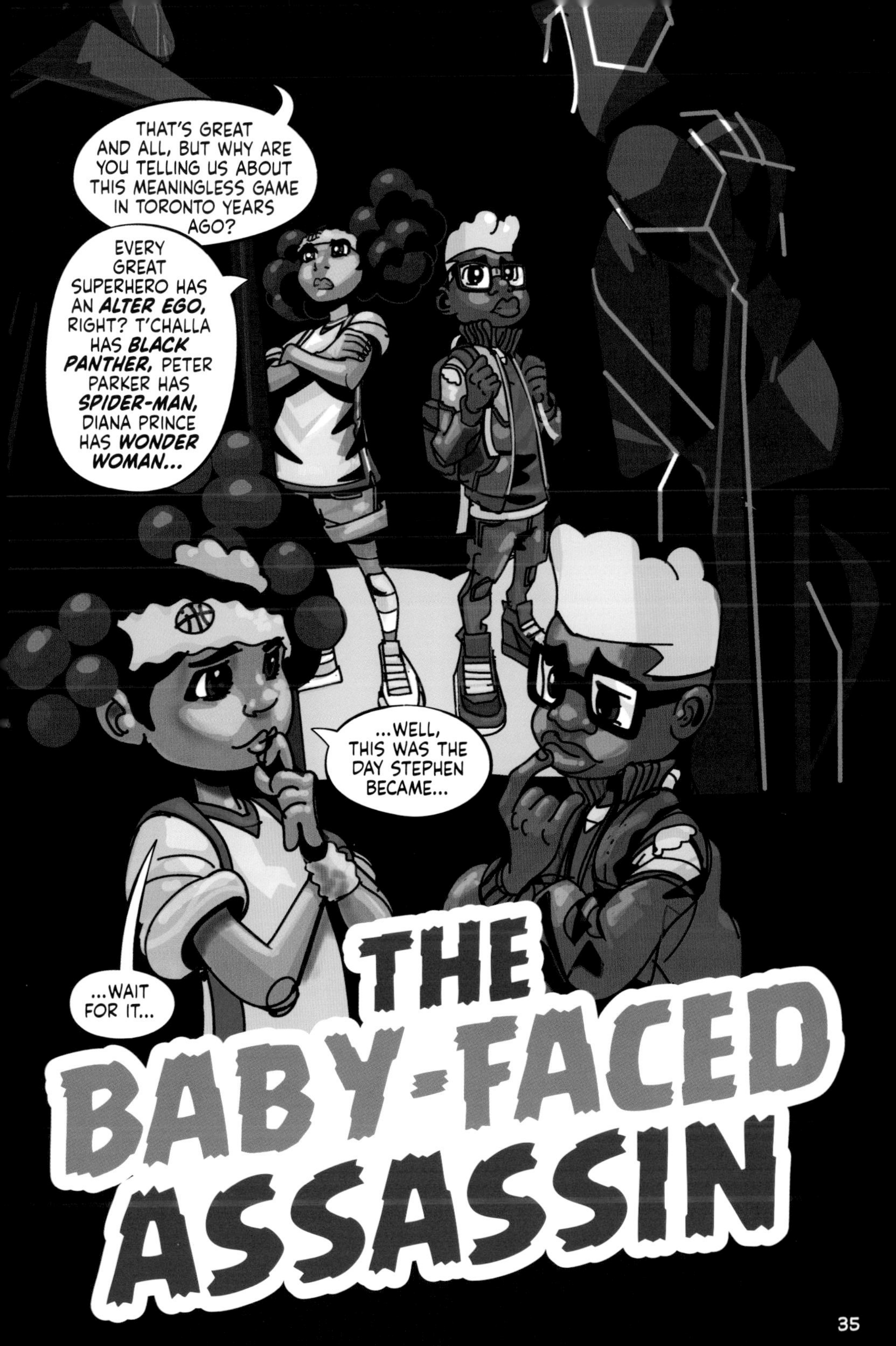
THAT'S GREAT AND ALL, BUT WHY ARE YOU TELLING US ABOUT THIS MEANINGLESS GAME IN TORONTO YEARS AGO?
EVERY GREAT SUPERHERO HAS AN ALTER EGO, RIGHT? T'CHALLA HAS BLACK PANTHER, PETER PARKER HAS SPIDER-MAN, DIANA PRINCE HAS WONDER WOMAN...
...WELL, THIS WAS THE DAY STEPHEN BECAME...
...WAIT FOR IT...
THE BABY-FACED ASSASSIN

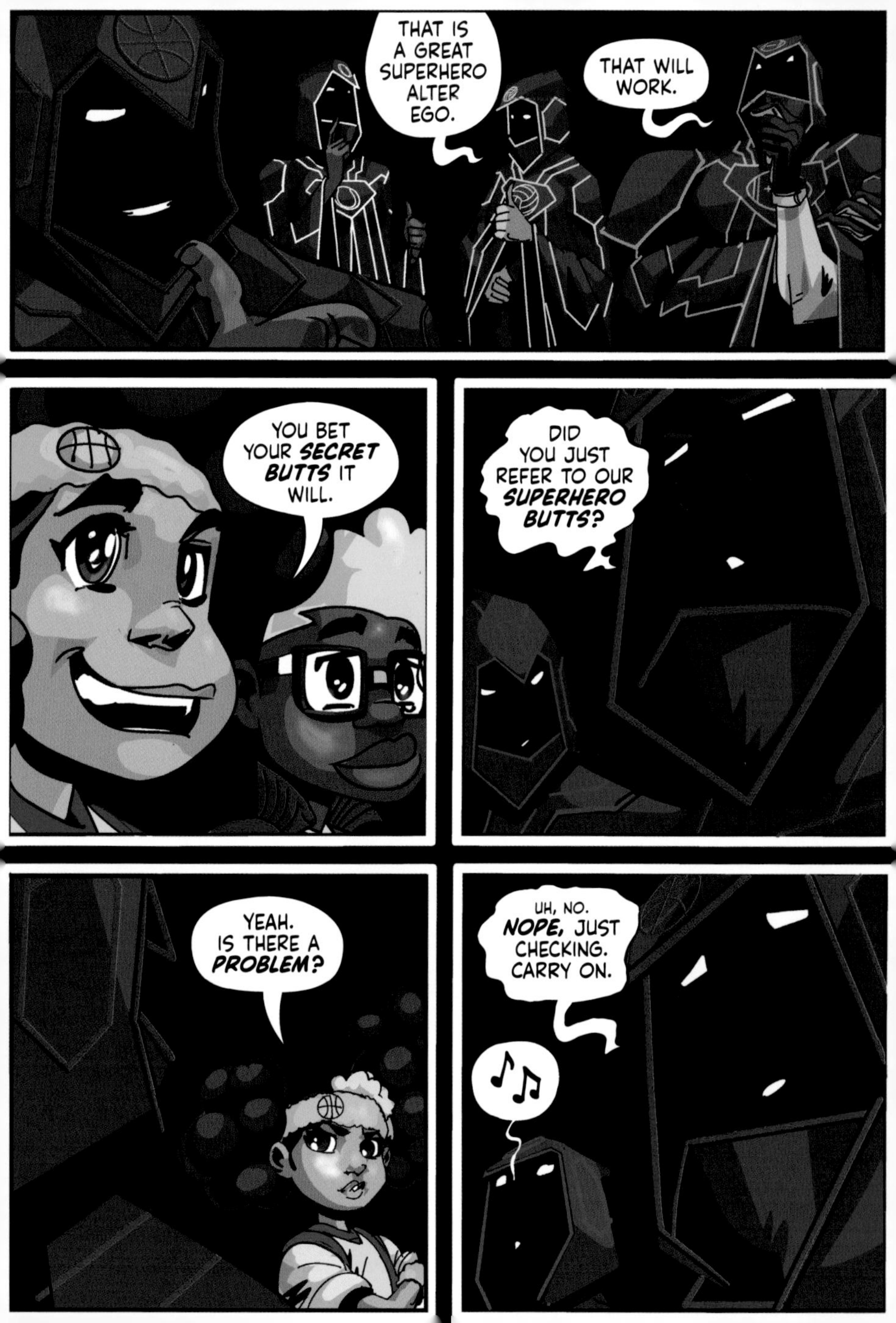
THAT IS A GREAT SUPERHERO ALTER EGO.
THAT WILL WORK.
YOU BET YOUR **SECRET BUTTS** IT WILL.
DID YOU JUST REFER TO OUR **SUPERHERO BUTTS?**
YEAH. IS THERE A **PROBLEM?**
UH, NO. **NOPE,** JUST CHECKING. CARRY ON.
♪♪

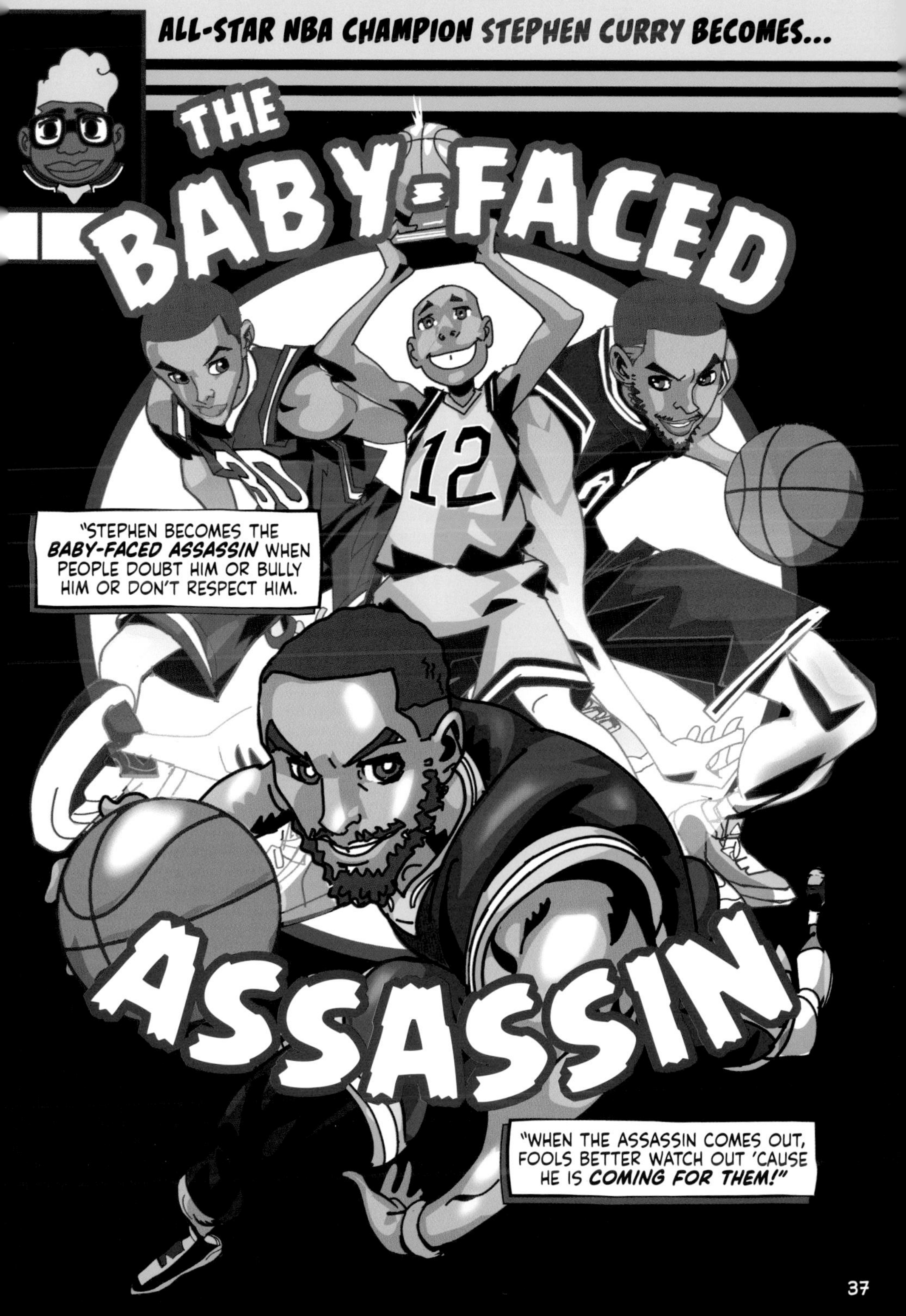
ALL-STAR NBA CHAMPION STEPHEN CURRY BECOMES...
THE BABY-FACED
"STEPHEN BECOMES THE BABY-FACED ASSASSIN WHEN PEOPLE DOUBT HIM OR BULLY HIM OR DON'T RESPECT HIM.
12
ASSASSIN
"WHEN THE ASSASSIN COMES OUT, FOOLS BETTER WATCH OUT 'CAUSE HE IS COMING FOR THEM!"

CHAPTER FOUR

NO ONE GETS TO
WRITE YOUR STORY

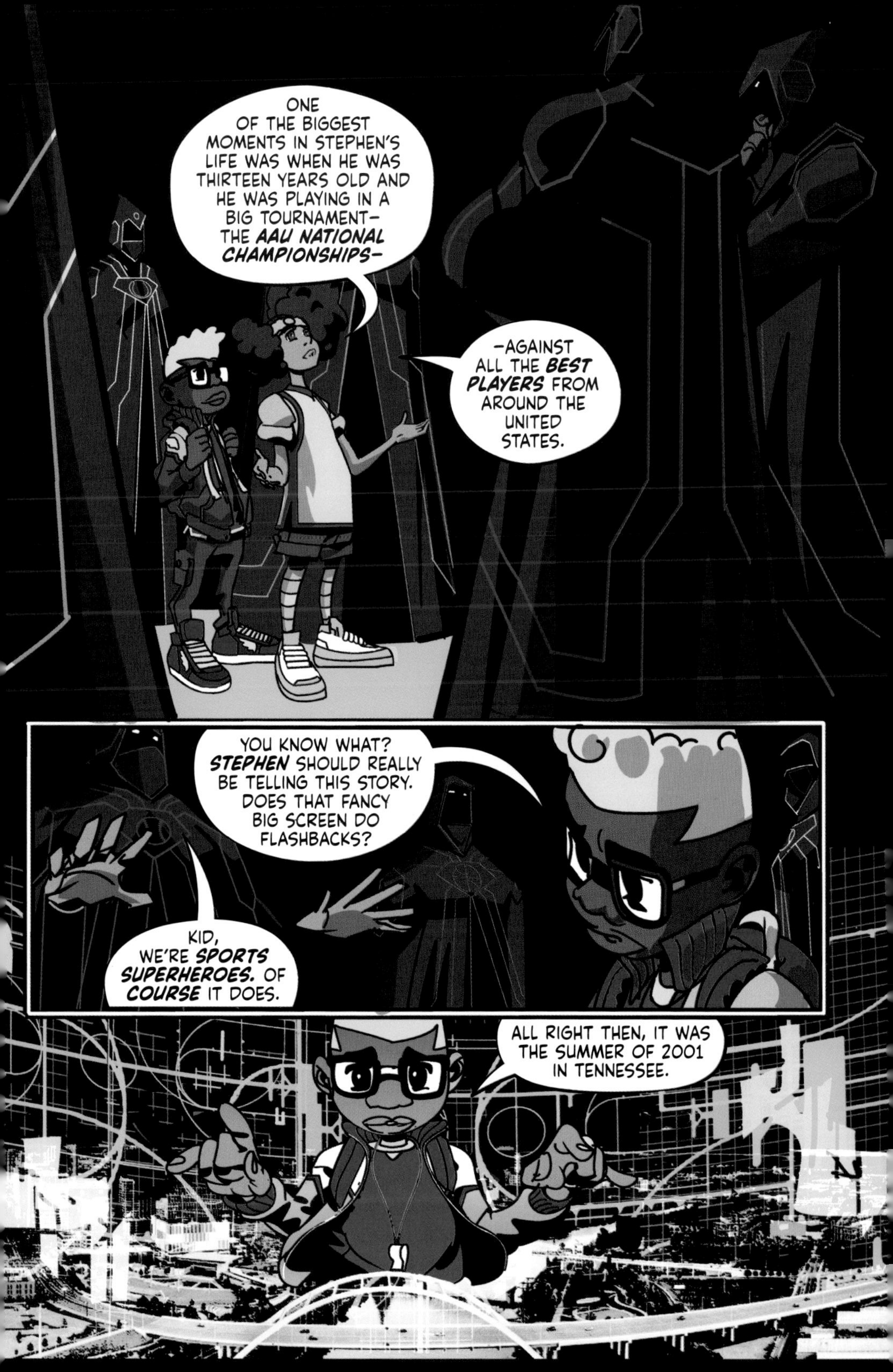
ONE OF THE BIGGEST MOMENTS IN STEPHEN'S LIFE WAS WHEN HE WAS THIRTEEN YEARS OLD AND HE WAS PLAYING IN A BIG TOURNAMENT— THE ***AAU NATIONAL CHAMPIONSHIPS***—
—AGAINST ALL THE ***BEST PLAYERS*** FROM AROUND THE UNITED STATES.
YOU KNOW WHAT? ***STEPHEN*** SHOULD REALLY BE TELLING THIS STORY. DOES THAT FANCY BIG SCREEN DO FLASHBACKS?
KID, WE'RE ***SPORTS SUPERHEROES.*** OF ***COURSE*** IT DOES.
ALL RIGHT THEN, IT WAS THE SUMMER OF 2001 IN TENNESSEE.

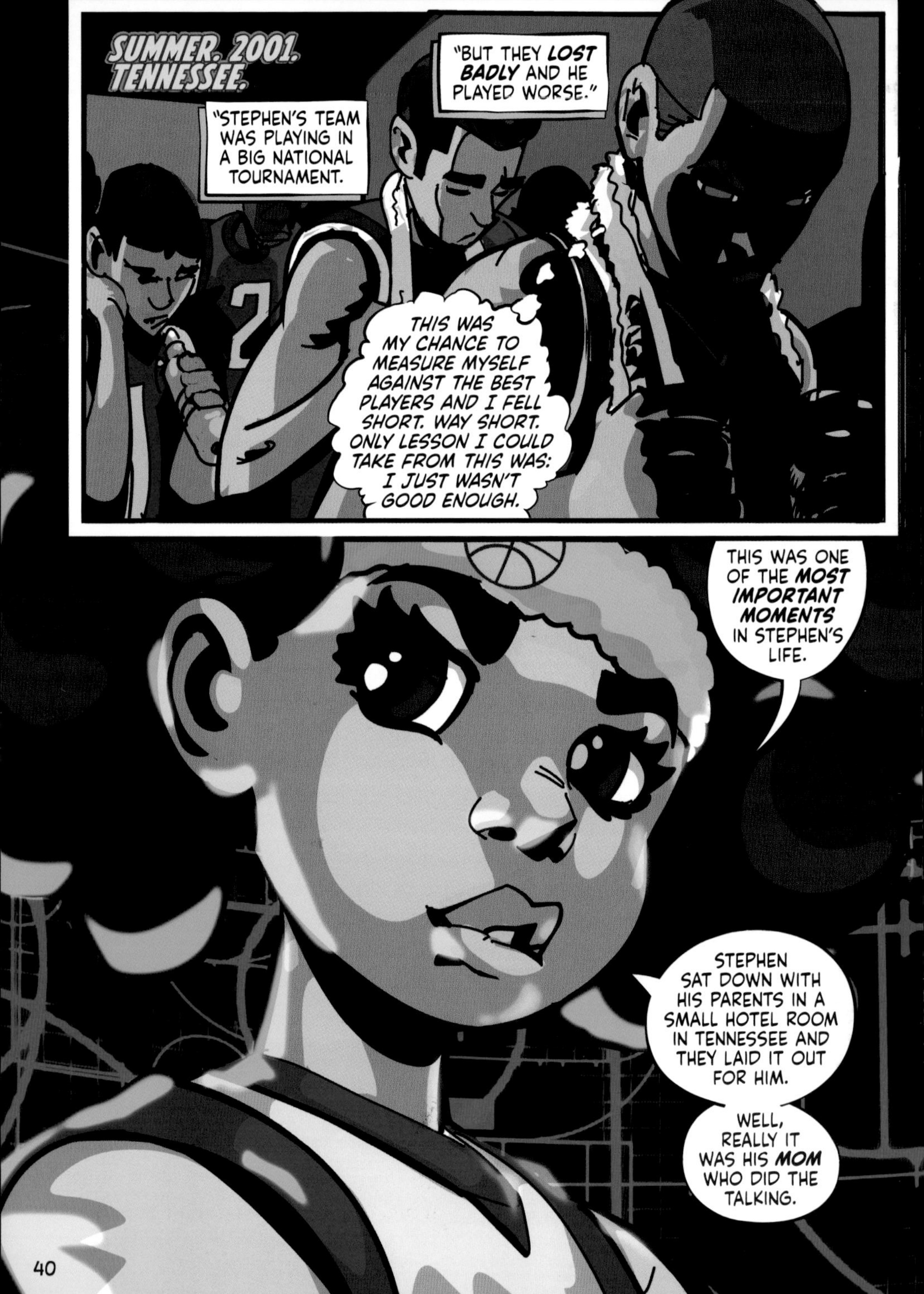
SUMMER. 2001. TENNESSEE.
"STEPHEN'S TEAM WAS PLAYING IN A BIG NATIONAL TOURNAMENT.
"BUT THEY LOST BADLY AND HE PLAYED WORSE."
THIS WAS MY CHANCE TO MEASURE MYSELF AGAINST THE BEST PLAYERS AND I FELL SHORT. WAY SHORT. ONLY LESSON I COULD TAKE FROM THIS WAS: I JUST WASN'T GOOD ENOUGH.
THIS WAS ONE OF THE MOST IMPORTANT MOMENTS IN STEPHEN'S LIFE.
STEPHEN SAT DOWN WITH HIS PARENTS IN A SMALL HOTEL ROOM IN TENNESSEE AND THEY LAID IT OUT FOR HIM.
WELL, REALLY IT WAS HIS MOM WHO DID THE TALKING.

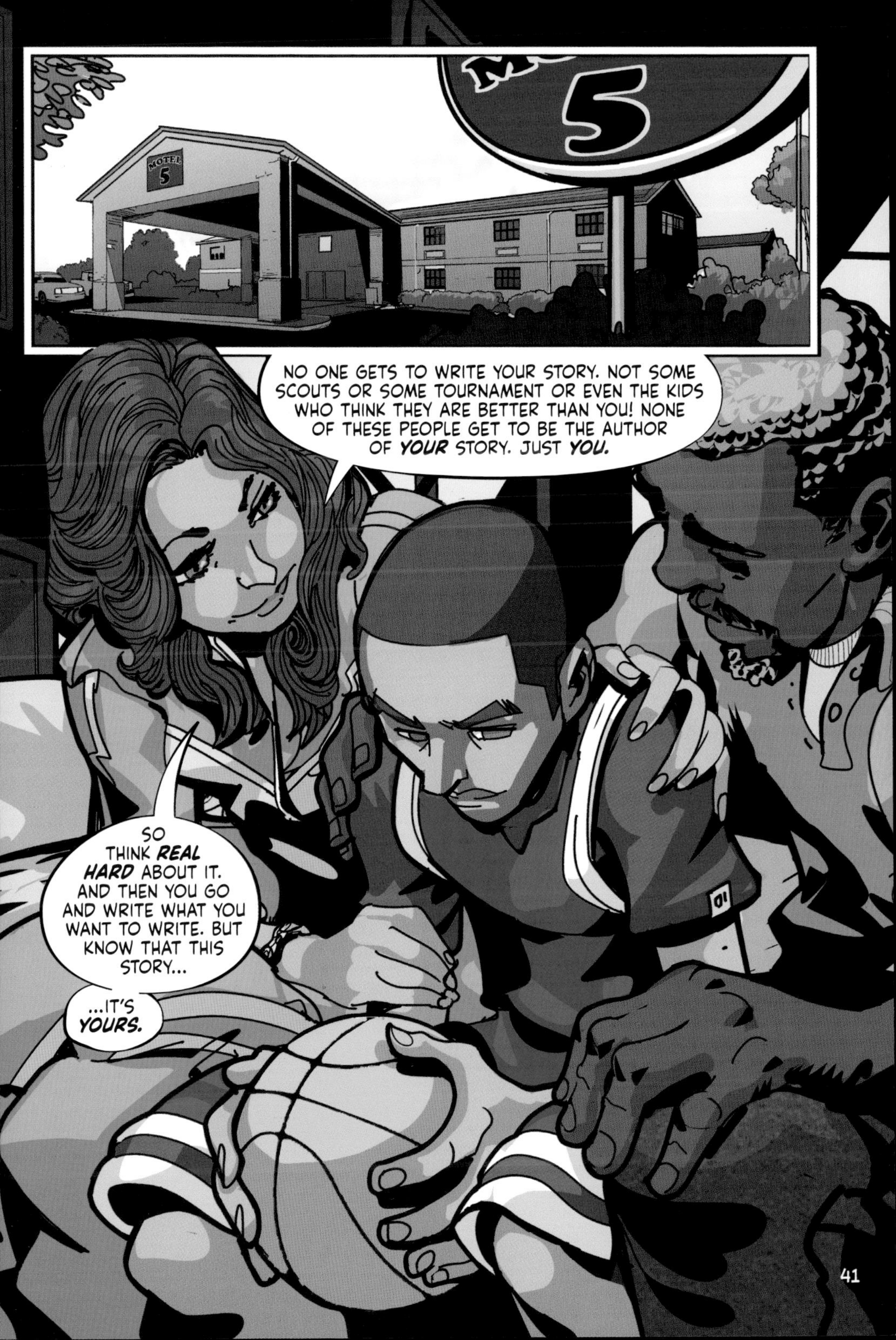
MOTEL 5
NO ONE GETS TO WRITE YOUR STORY. NOT SOME SCOUTS OR SOME TOURNAMENT OR EVEN THE KIDS WHO THINK THEY ARE BETTER THAN YOU! NONE OF THESE PEOPLE GET TO BE THE AUTHOR OF ***YOUR*** STORY. JUST ***YOU.***
SO THINK ***REAL HARD*** ABOUT IT. AND THEN YOU GO AND WRITE WHAT YOU WANT TO WRITE. BUT KNOW THAT THIS STORY...
...IT'S ***YOURS.***

CHAPTER FIVE

THE SUMMER
OF TEARS

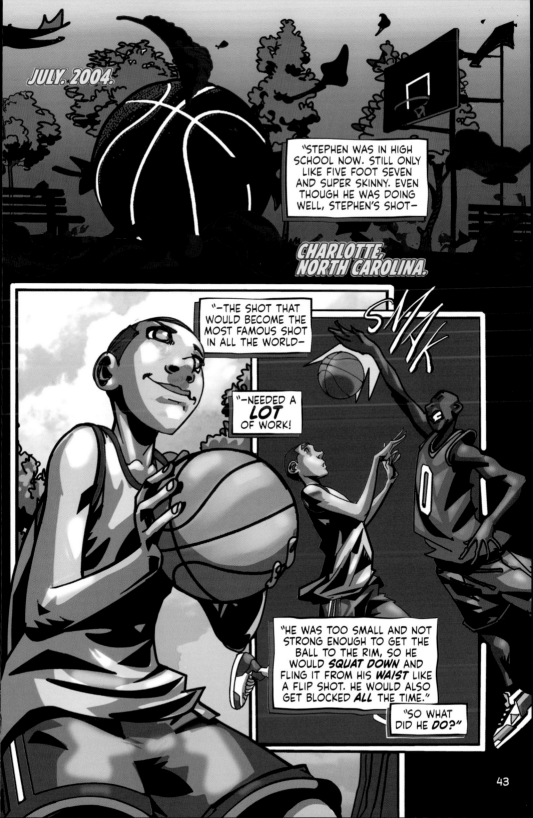

JULY, 2004,

"STEPHEN WAS IN HIGH SCHOOL NOW. STILL ONLY LIKE FIVE FOOT SEVEN AND SUPER SKINNY. EVEN THOUGH HE WAS DOING WELL, STEPHEN'S SHOT—

CHARLOTTE, NORTH CAROLINA.

"—THE SHOT THAT WOULD BECOME THE MOST FAMOUS SHOT IN ALL THE WORLD—

"—NEEDED A *LOT* OF WORK!

SMAK

"HE WAS TOO SMALL AND NOT STRONG ENOUGH TO GET THE BALL TO THE RIM, SO HE WOULD *SQUAT DOWN* AND FLING IT FROM HIS *WAIST* LIKE A FLIP SHOT. HE WOULD ALSO GET BLOCKED *ALL* THE TIME."

"SO WHAT DID HE *DO?*"

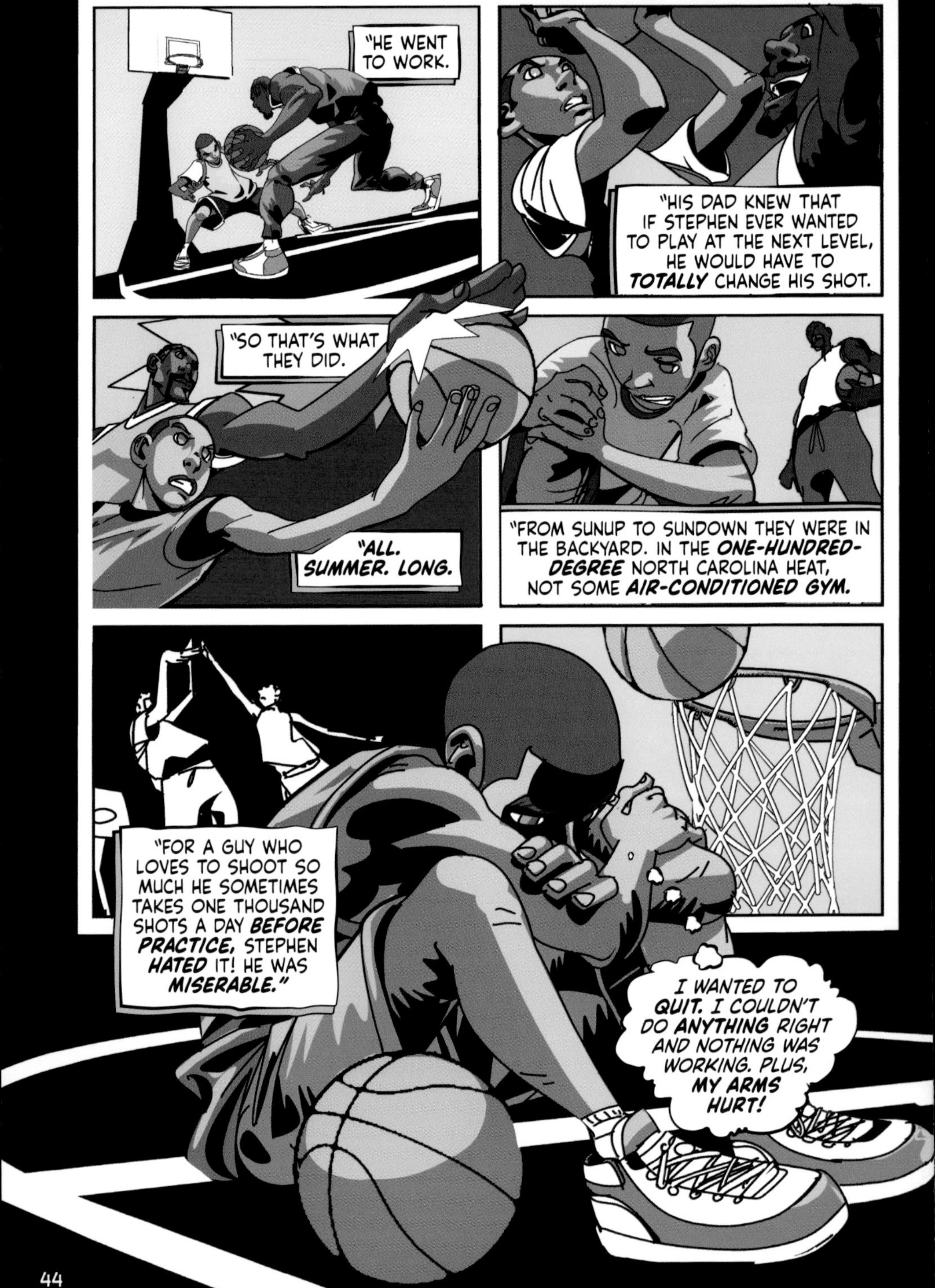
"HE WENT TO WORK.
"HIS DAD KNEW THAT IF STEPHEN EVER WANTED TO PLAY AT THE NEXT LEVEL, HE WOULD HAVE TO ***TOTALLY*** CHANGE HIS SHOT.
"SO THAT'S WHAT THEY DID.
"ALL. SUMMER. LONG.
"FROM SUNUP TO SUNDOWN THEY WERE IN THE BACKYARD. IN THE ***ONE-HUNDRED-DEGREE*** NORTH CAROLINA HEAT, NOT SOME ***AIR-CONDITIONED GYM.***
"FOR A GUY WHO LOVES TO SHOOT SO MUCH HE SOMETIMES TAKES ONE THOUSAND SHOTS A DAY ***BEFORE PRACTICE,*** STEPHEN ***HATED*** IT! HE WAS ***MISERABLE."***
I WANTED TO ***QUIT.*** *I COULDN'T DO* ***ANYTHING*** *RIGHT AND NOTHING WAS WORKING. PLUS,* ***MY ARMS HURT!***

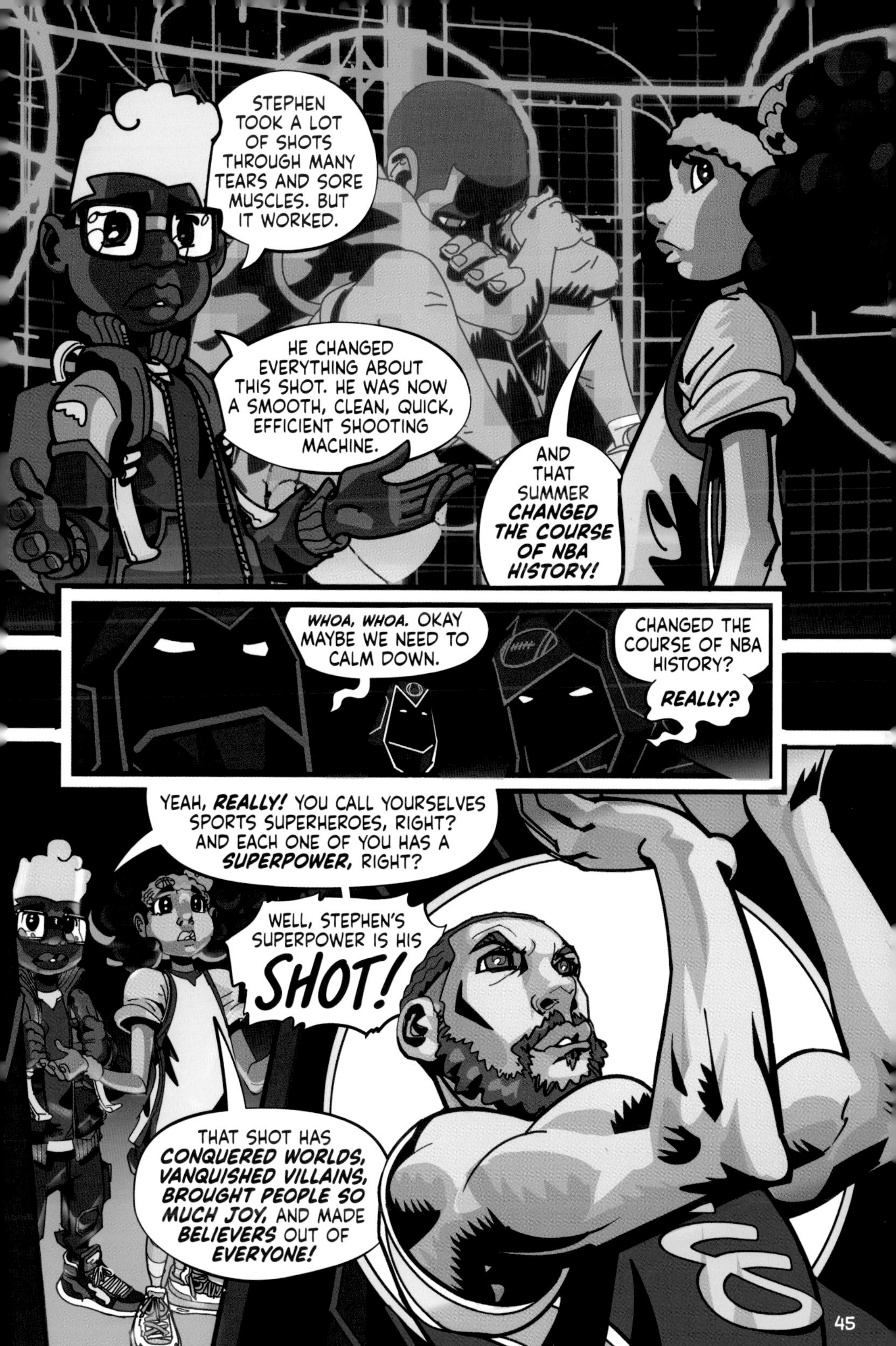
STEPHEN TOOK A LOT OF SHOTS THROUGH MANY TEARS AND SORE MUSCLES. BUT IT WORKED.
HE CHANGED EVERYTHING ABOUT THIS SHOT. HE WAS NOW A SMOOTH, CLEAN, QUICK, EFFICIENT SHOOTING MACHINE.
AND THAT SUMMER ***CHANGED THE COURSE OF NBA HISTORY!***
WHOA, WHOA. OKAY MAYBE WE NEED TO CALM DOWN.
CHANGED THE COURSE OF NBA HISTORY?
REALLY?
YEAH, ***REALLY!*** YOU CALL YOURSELVES SPORTS SUPERHEROES, RIGHT? AND EACH ONE OF YOU HAS A ***SUPERPOWER,*** RIGHT?
WELL, STEPHEN'S SUPERPOWER IS HIS
SHOT!
THAT SHOT HAS ***CONQUERED WORLDS, VANQUISHED VILLAINS, BROUGHT PEOPLE SO MUCH JOY,*** AND MADE ***BELIEVERS*** OUT OF ***EVERYONE!***

CHAPTER SIX

THE STRAIGHT-UP STATS

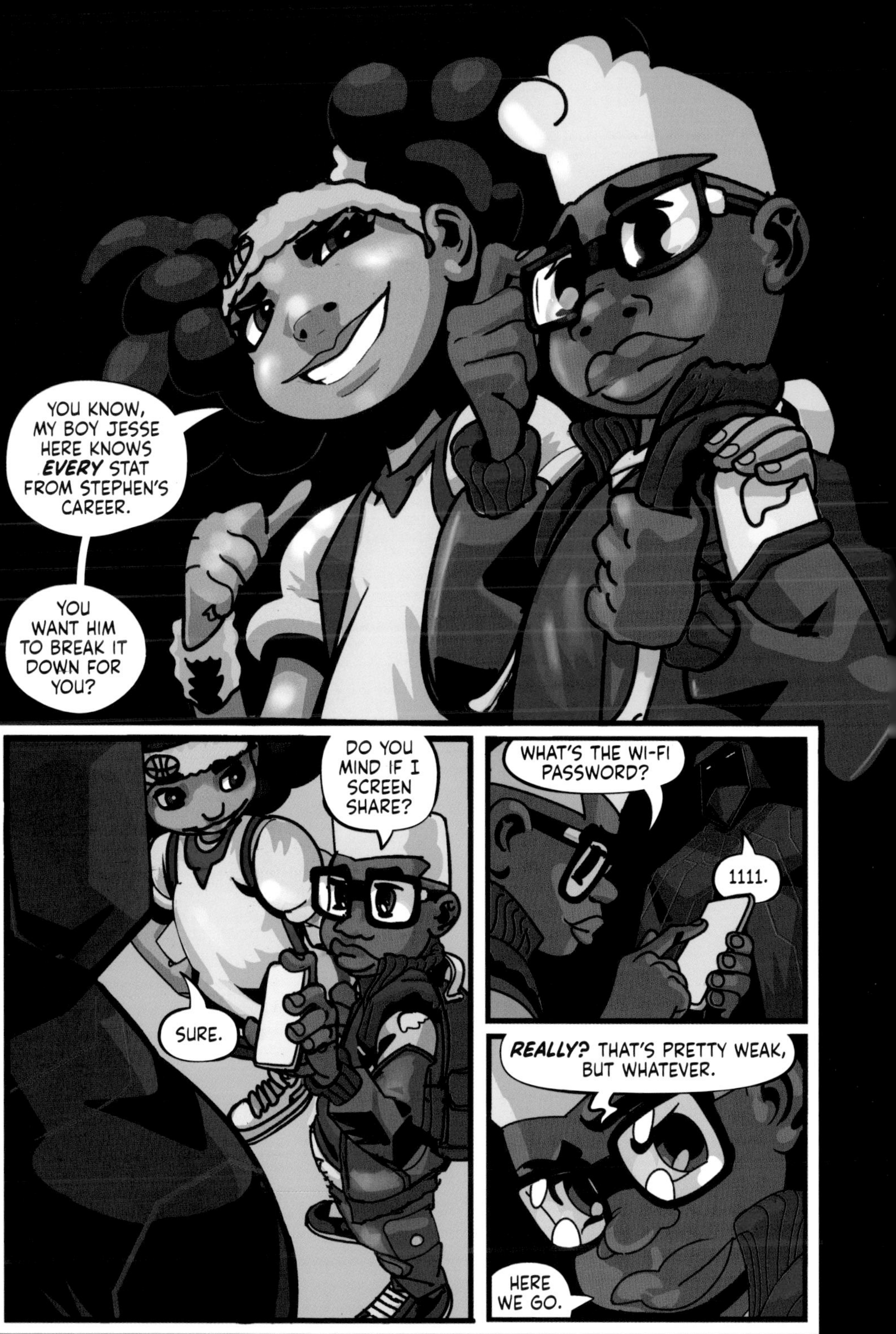
YOU KNOW, MY BOY JESSE HERE KNOWS **EVERY** STAT FROM STEPHEN'S CAREER.
YOU WANT HIM TO BREAK IT DOWN FOR YOU?
DO YOU MIND IF I SCREEN SHARE?
SURE.
WHAT'S THE WI-FI PASSWORD?
1111.
REALLY? THAT'S PRETTY WEAK, BUT WHATEVER.
HERE WE GO.

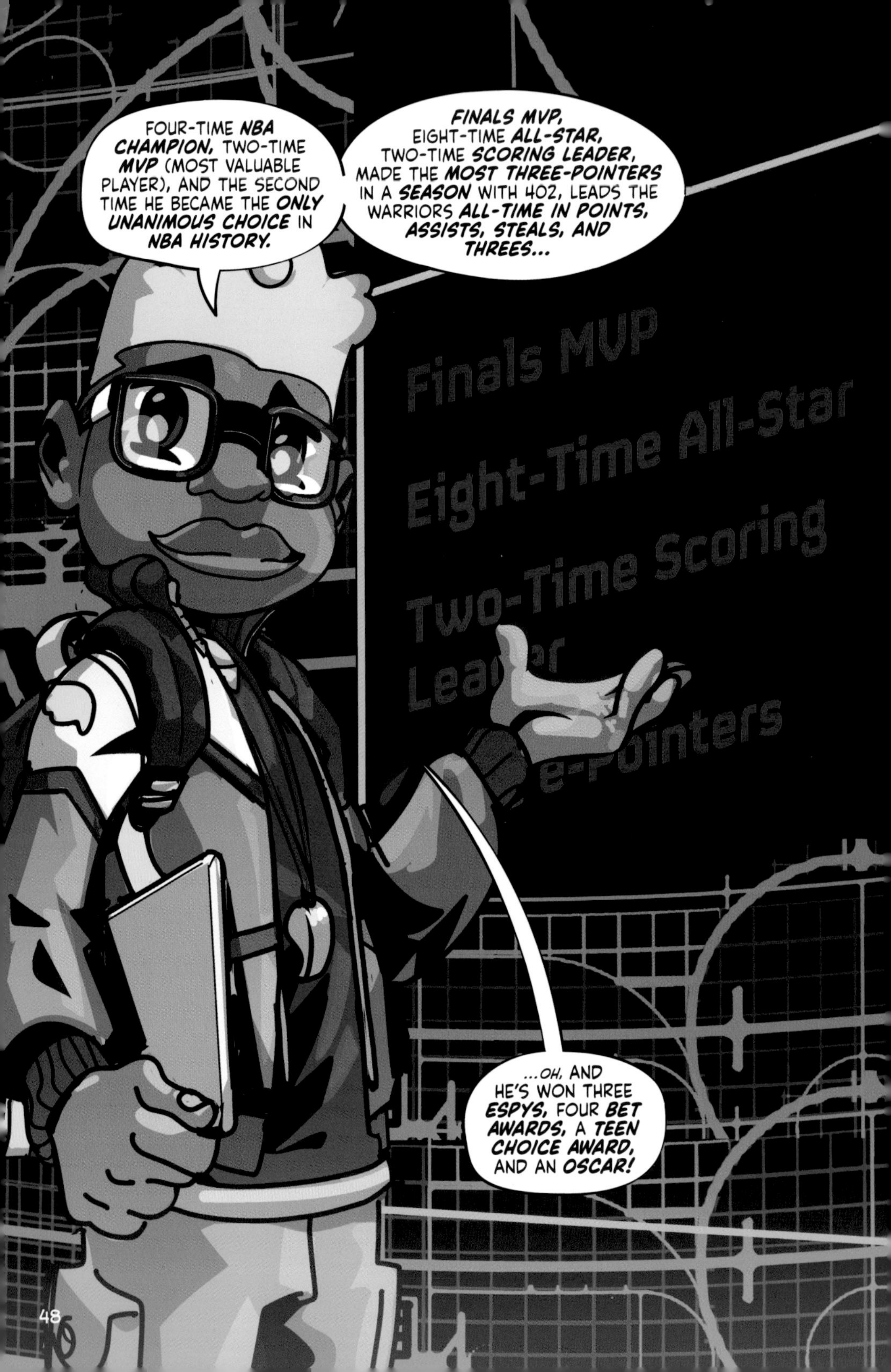
FOUR-TIME NBA CHAMPION, TWO-TIME MVP (MOST VALUABLE PLAYER), AND THE SECOND TIME HE BECAME THE ONLY UNANIMOUS CHOICE IN NBA HISTORY.
FINALS MVP, EIGHT-TIME ALL-STAR, TWO-TIME SCORING LEADER, MADE THE MOST THREE-POINTERS IN A SEASON WITH 402, LEADS THE WARRIORS ALL-TIME IN POINTS, ASSISTS, STEALS, AND THREES...
Finals MVP
Eight-Time All-Star
Two-Time Scoring
...OH, AND HE'S WON THREE ESPYS, FOUR BET AWARDS, A TEEN CHOICE AWARD, AND AN OSCAR!

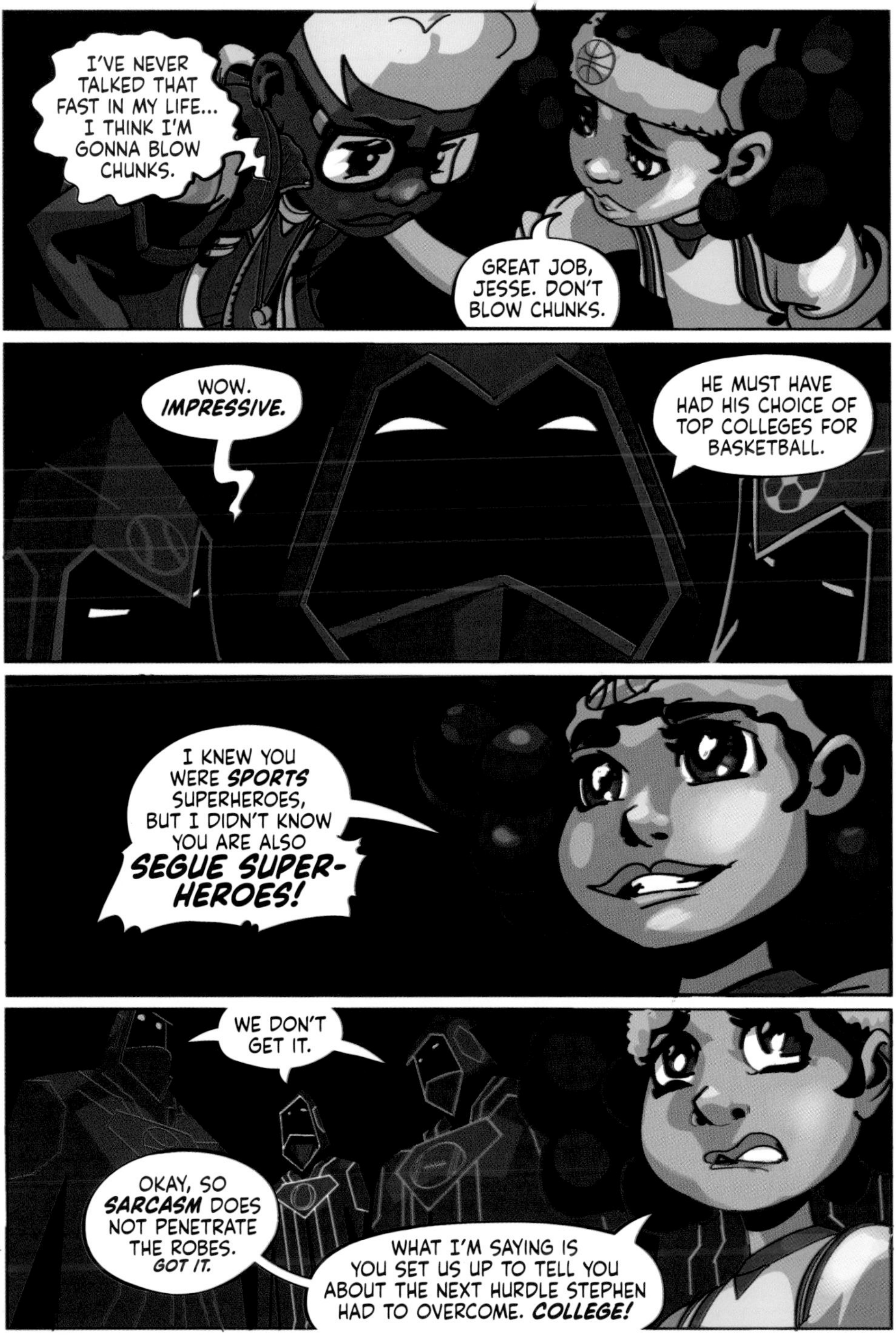
I'VE NEVER TALKED THAT FAST IN MY LIFE... I THINK I'M GONNA BLOW CHUNKS.
GREAT JOB, JESSE. DON'T BLOW CHUNKS.
WOW. *IMPRESSIVE.*
HE MUST HAVE HAD HIS CHOICE OF TOP COLLEGES FOR BASKETBALL.
I KNEW YOU WERE *SPORTS* SUPERHEROES, BUT I DIDN'T KNOW YOU ARE ALSO **SEGUE SUPER-HEROES!**
WE DON'T GET IT.
OKAY, SO *SARCASM* DOES NOT PENETRATE THE ROBES. *GOT IT.*
WHAT I'M SAYING IS YOU SET US UP TO TELL YOU ABOUT THE NEXT HURDLE STEPHEN HAD TO OVERCOME. *COLLEGE!*

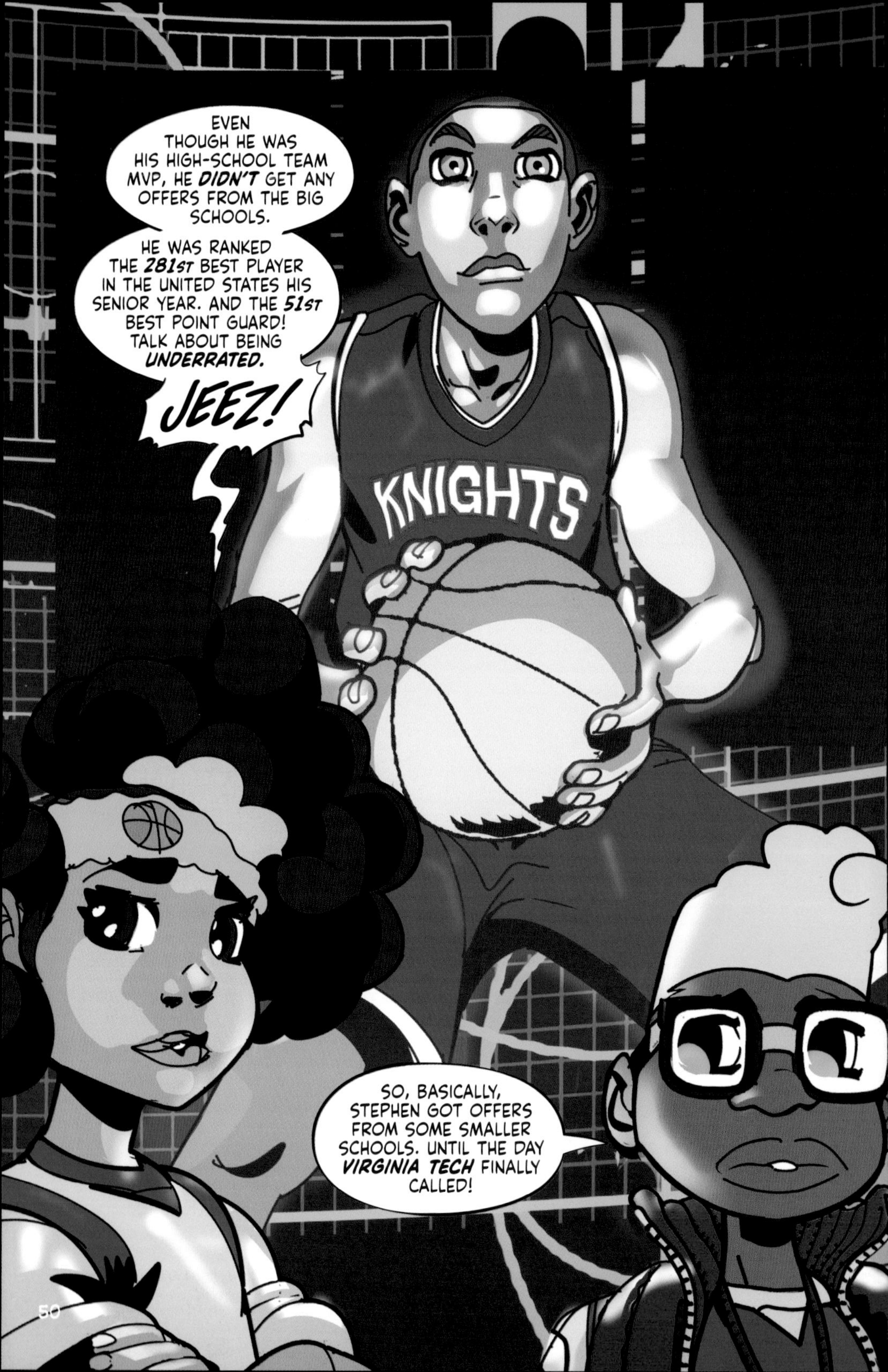
EVEN THOUGH HE WAS HIS HIGH-SCHOOL TEAM MVP, HE ***DIDN'T*** GET ANY OFFERS FROM THE BIG SCHOOLS.
HE WAS RANKED THE ***281ST*** BEST PLAYER IN THE UNITED STATES HIS SENIOR YEAR. AND THE ***51ST*** BEST POINT GUARD! TALK ABOUT BEING ***UNDERRATED.***
JEEZ!
KNIGHTS
SO, BASICALLY, STEPHEN GOT OFFERS FROM SOME SMALLER SCHOOLS. UNTIL THE DAY ***VIRGINIA TECH*** FINALLY CALLED!

CHAPTER
SEVEN

THE MEETING
IN THE CAFETERIA

"SO VIRGINIA TECH IS IN THE *ATLANTIC COAST CONFERENCE,* THE ACC. IT'S THE HOME OF COLLEGE BASKETBALL BECAUSE MANY CONSIDER IT THE *BEST* CONFERENCE."

"THIS WAS STEPHEN'S *DREAM* SCHOOL. IT WAS WHERE BOTH HIS PARENTS HAD BEEN STAR ATHLETES. AND NOW THEY WANTED TO COME TO HIS HIGH SCHOOL AND MEET HIM.

"SO STEPHEN MADE A *PLAN.*"

YOU KNOW WHAT? WE SHOULD REALLY LET *STEPHEN* TELL THIS STORY.

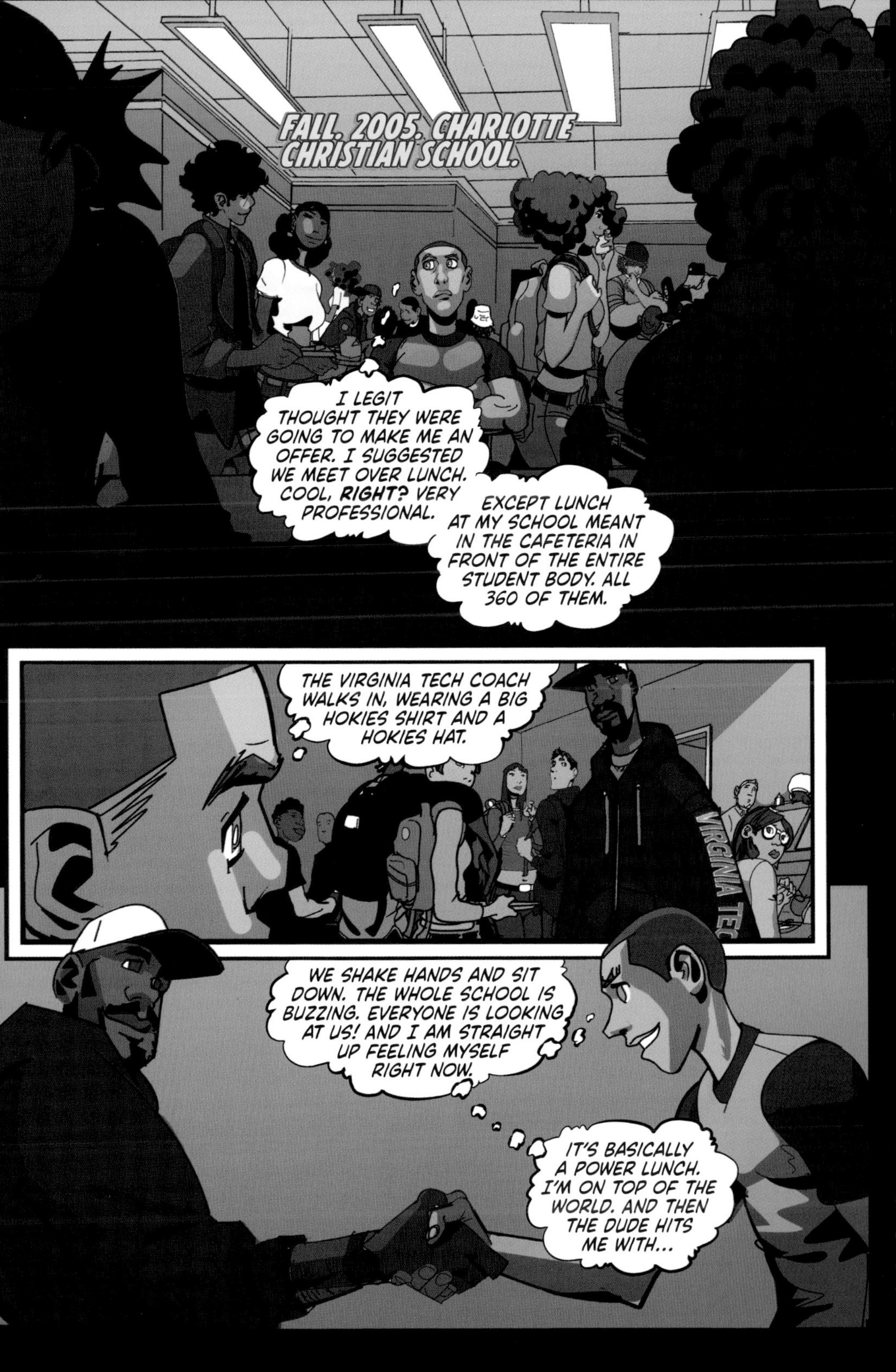
FALL. 2005. CHARLOTTE CHRISTIAN SCHOOL.
I LEGIT THOUGHT THEY WERE GOING TO MAKE ME AN OFFER. I SUGGESTED WE MEET OVER LUNCH. COOL, **RIGHT?** VERY PROFESSIONAL.
EXCEPT LUNCH AT MY SCHOOL MEANT IN THE CAFETERIA IN FRONT OF THE ENTIRE STUDENT BODY. ALL 360 OF THEM.
THE VIRGINIA TECH COACH WALKS IN, WEARING A BIG HOKIES SHIRT AND A HOKIES HAT.
VIRGINIA TEC
WE SHAKE HANDS AND SIT DOWN. THE WHOLE SCHOOL IS BUZZING. EVERYONE IS LOOKING AT US! AND I AM STRAIGHT UP FEELING MYSELF RIGHT NOW.
IT'S BASICALLY A POWER LUNCH. I'M ON TOP OF THE WORLD. AND THEN THE DUDE HITS ME WITH...

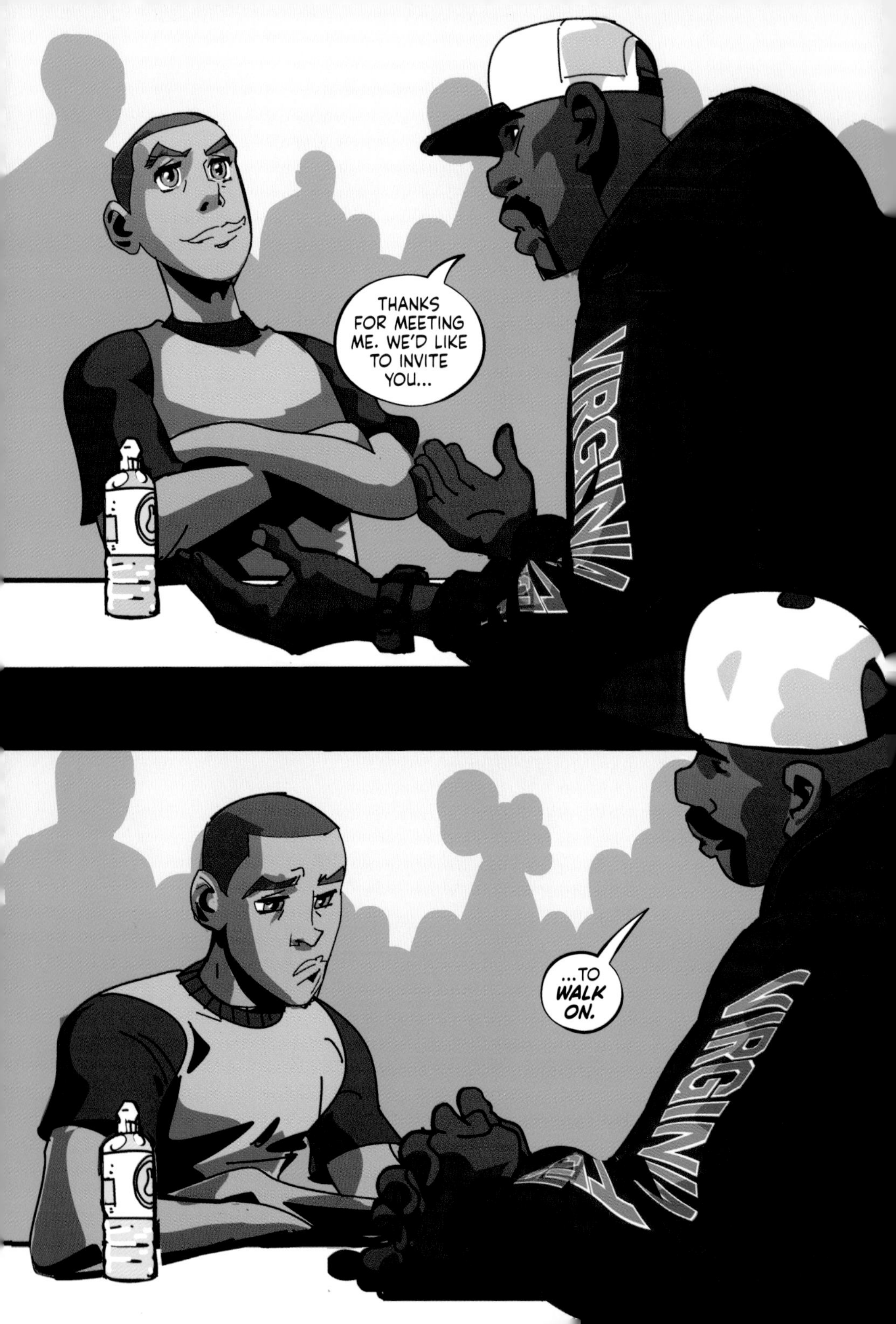
THANKS FOR MEETING ME. WE'D LIKE TO INVITE YOU...
...TO WALK ON.
VIRGINIA
VIRGINIA

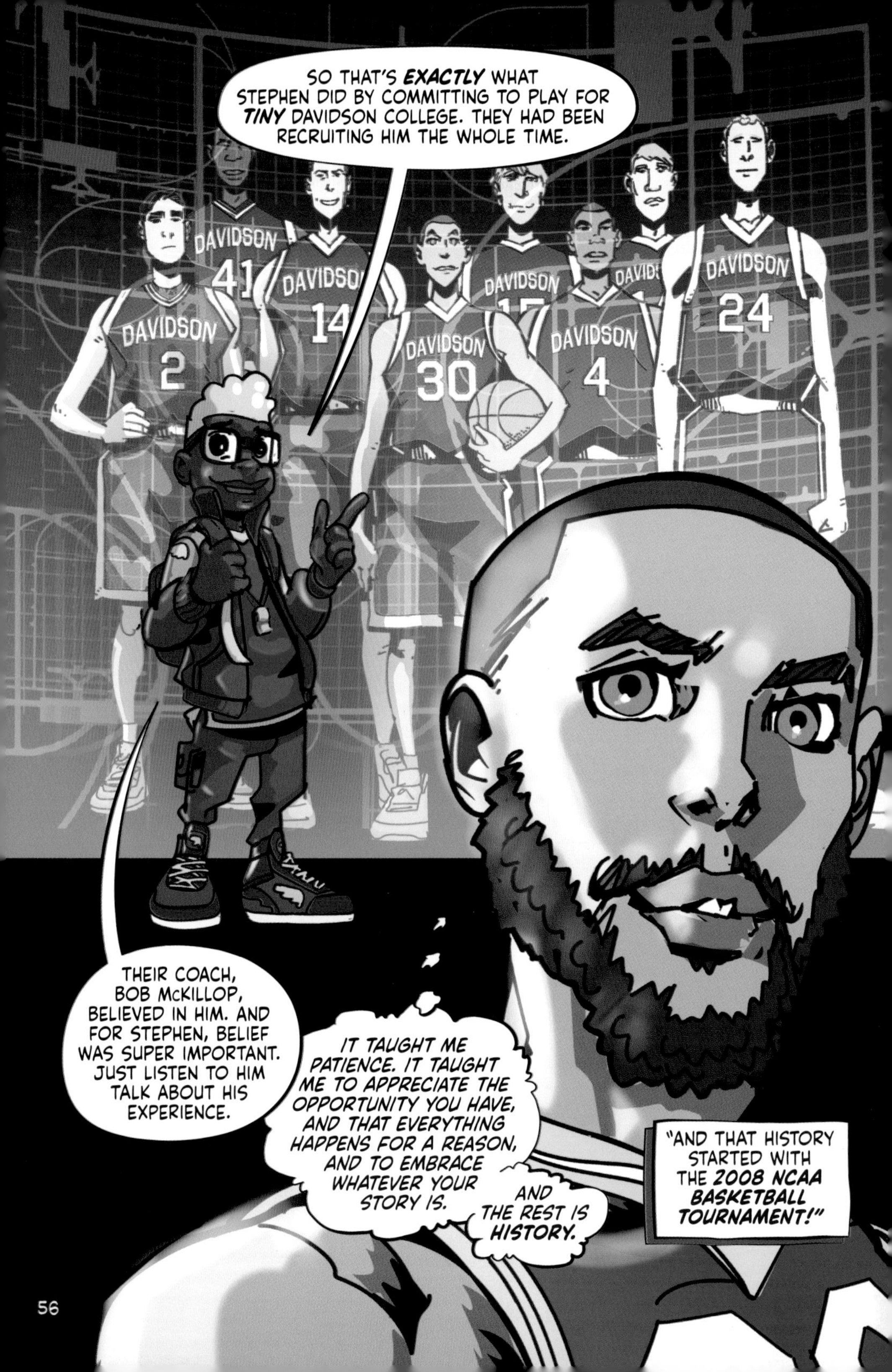

SO THAT'S **EXACTLY** WHAT STEPHEN DID BY COMMITTING TO PLAY FOR ***TINY*** DAVIDSON COLLEGE. THEY HAD BEEN RECRUITING HIM THE WHOLE TIME.
DAVIDSON 41
DAVIDSON 14
DAVIDSON 2
DAVIDSON 30
DAVIDSON
DAVIDSON 4
DAVIDSON 24
THEIR COACH, BOB McKILLOP, BELIEVED IN HIM. AND FOR STEPHEN, BELIEF WAS SUPER IMPORTANT. JUST LISTEN TO HIM TALK ABOUT HIS EXPERIENCE.
IT TAUGHT ME PATIENCE. IT TAUGHT ME TO APPRECIATE THE OPPORTUNITY YOU HAVE, AND THAT EVERYTHING HAPPENS FOR A REASON, AND TO EMBRACE WHATEVER YOUR STORY IS.
*AND THE REST IS **HISTORY.***
"AND THAT HISTORY STARTED WITH THE ***2008 NCAA BASKETBALL TOURNAMENT!***"

CHAPTER EIGHT

THE WORLD MEETS
STEPHEN CURRY

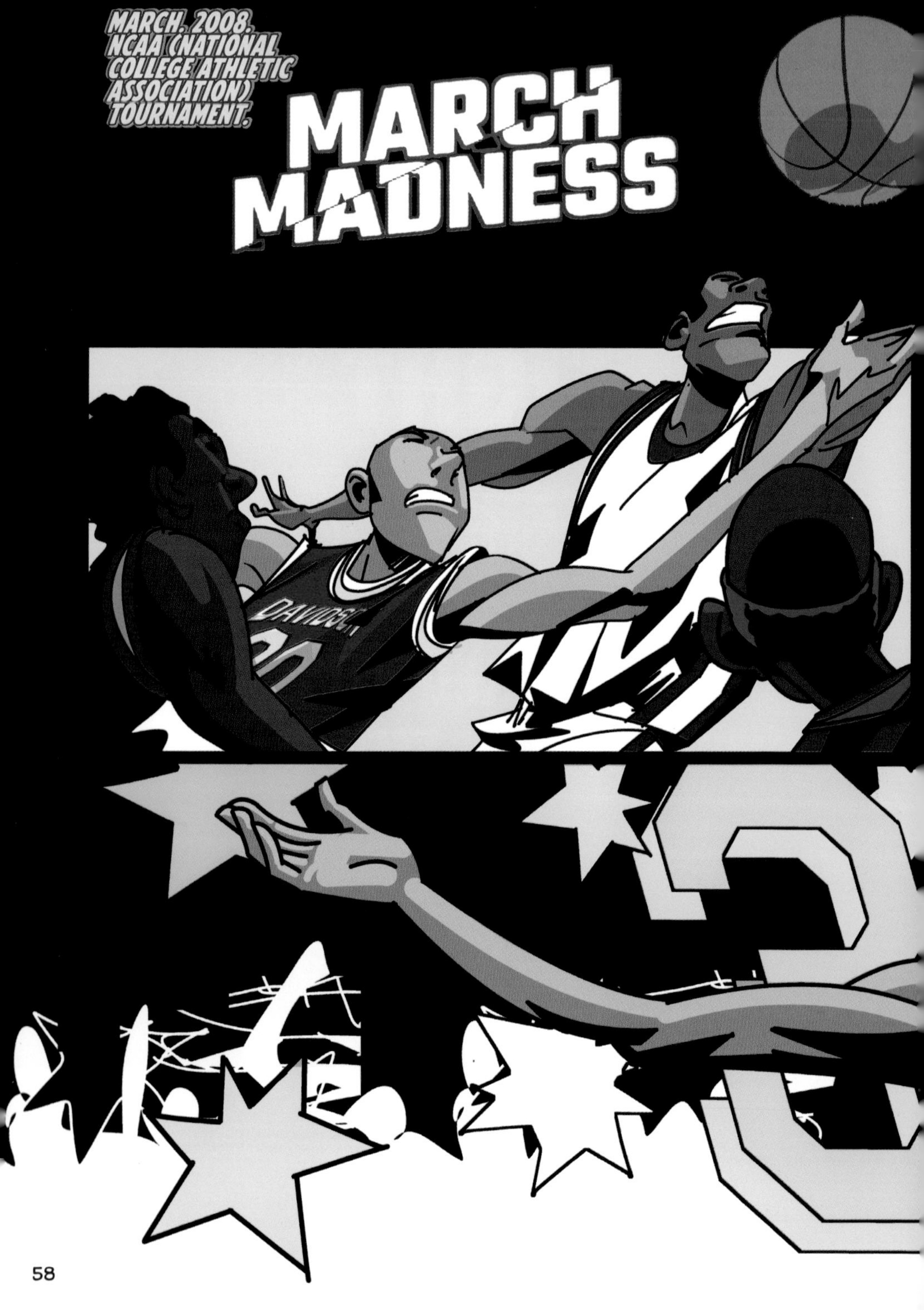

MARCH, 2008.
NCAA (NATIONAL COLLEGE ATHLETIC ASSOCIATION) TOURNAMENT.
MARCH MADNESS
DAVIDSON

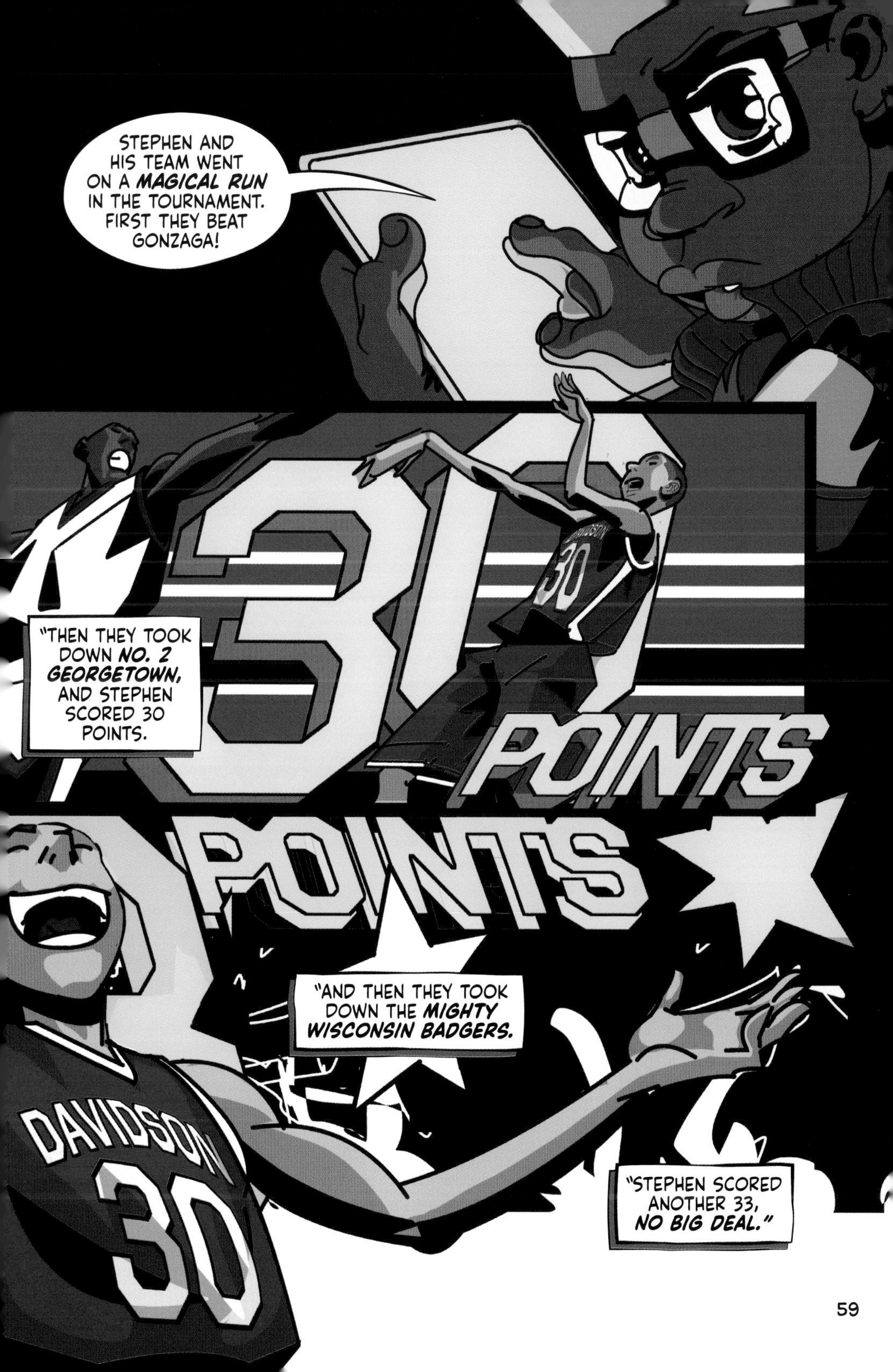

STEPHEN AND HIS TEAM WENT ON A *MAGICAL RUN* IN THE TOURNAMENT. FIRST THEY BEAT GONZAGA!
"THEN THEY TOOK DOWN ***NO. 2 GEORGETOWN,*** AND STEPHEN SCORED 30 POINTS.
DAVIDSON
30
30
POINTS
POINTS
"AND THEN THEY TOOK DOWN THE ***MIGHTY WISCONSIN BADGERS.***
"STEPHEN SCORED ANOTHER 33, ***NO BIG DEAL."***
DAVIDSON
30

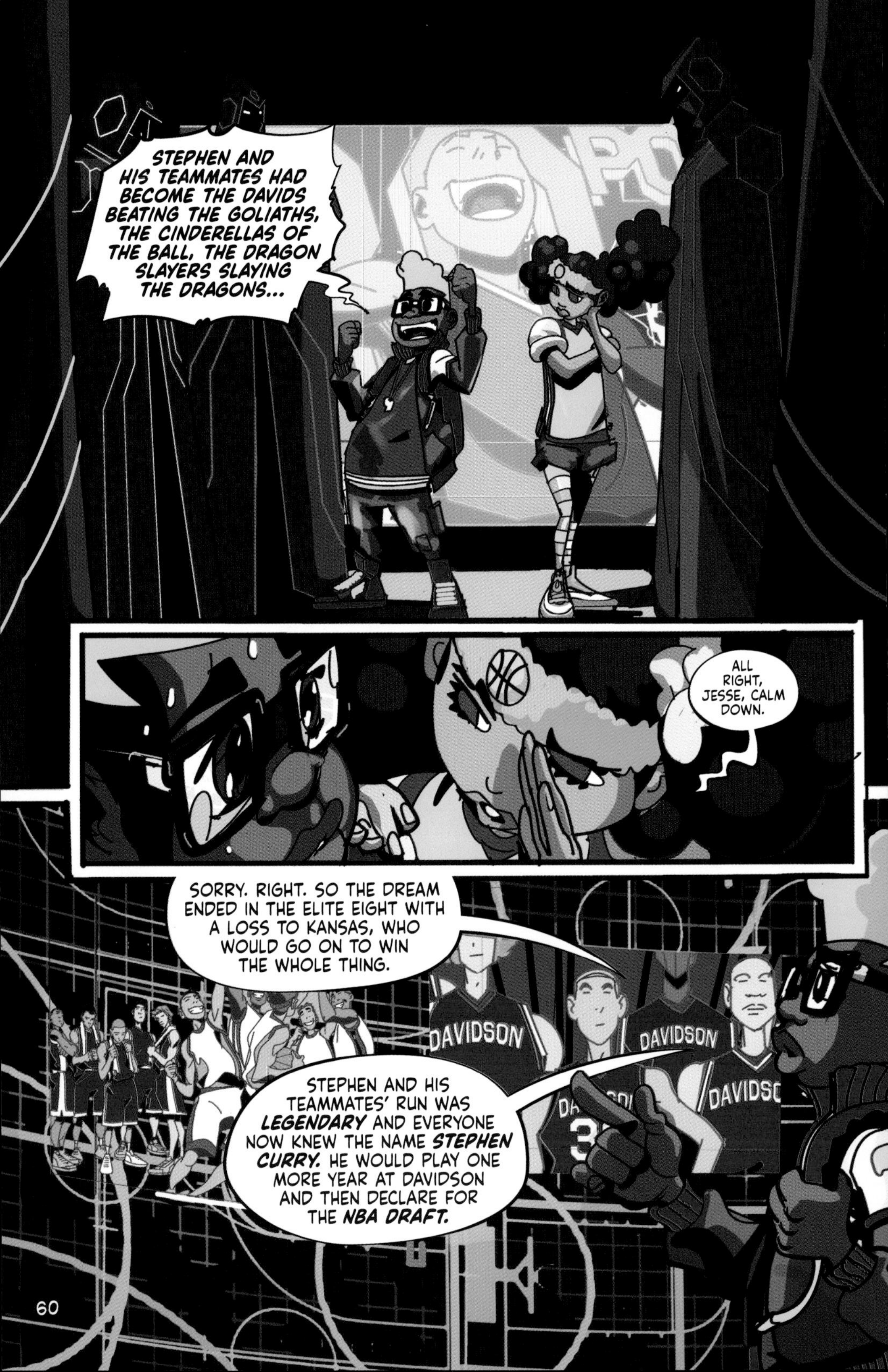
STEPHEN AND HIS TEAMMATES HAD BECOME THE DAVIDS BEATING THE GOLIATHS, THE CINDERELLAS OF THE BALL, THE DRAGON SLAYERS SLAYING THE DRAGONS...
ALL RIGHT, JESSE, CALM DOWN.
SORRY. RIGHT. SO THE DREAM ENDED IN THE ELITE EIGHT WITH A LOSS TO KANSAS, WHO WOULD GO ON TO WIN THE WHOLE THING.
DAVIDSON
DAVIDSON
DAVIDSON
STEPHEN AND HIS TEAMMATES' RUN WAS ***LEGENDARY*** AND EVERYONE NOW KNEW THE NAME ***STEPHEN CURRY.*** HE WOULD PLAY ONE MORE YEAR AT DAVIDSON AND THEN DECLARE FOR THE ***NBA DRAFT.***

CHAPTER NINE

THE NBA!

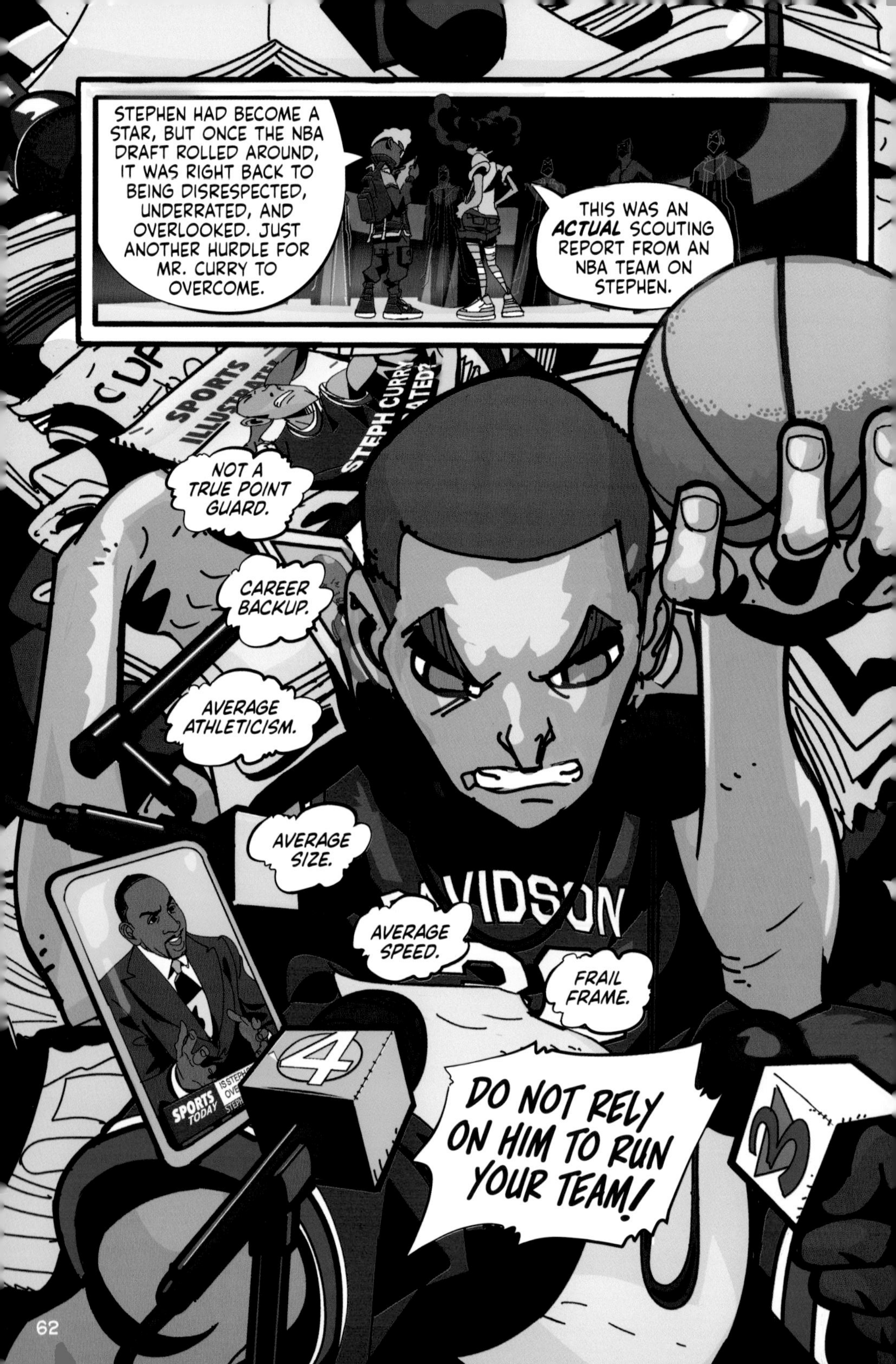
STEPHEN HAD BECOME A STAR, BUT ONCE THE NBA DRAFT ROLLED AROUND, IT WAS RIGHT BACK TO BEING DISRESPECTED, UNDERRATED, AND OVERLOOKED. JUST ANOTHER HURDLE FOR MR. CURRY TO OVERCOME.
THIS WAS AN *ACTUAL* SCOUTING REPORT FROM AN NBA TEAM ON STEPHEN.
SPORTS ILLUSTRATED
STEPH CURRY ...ATED?
NOT A TRUE POINT GUARD.
CAREER BACKUP.
AVERAGE ATHLETICISM.
AVERAGE SIZE.
DAVIDSON
AVERAGE SPEED.
FRAIL FRAME.
SPORTS TODAY
DO NOT RELY ON HIM TO RUN YOUR TEAM!

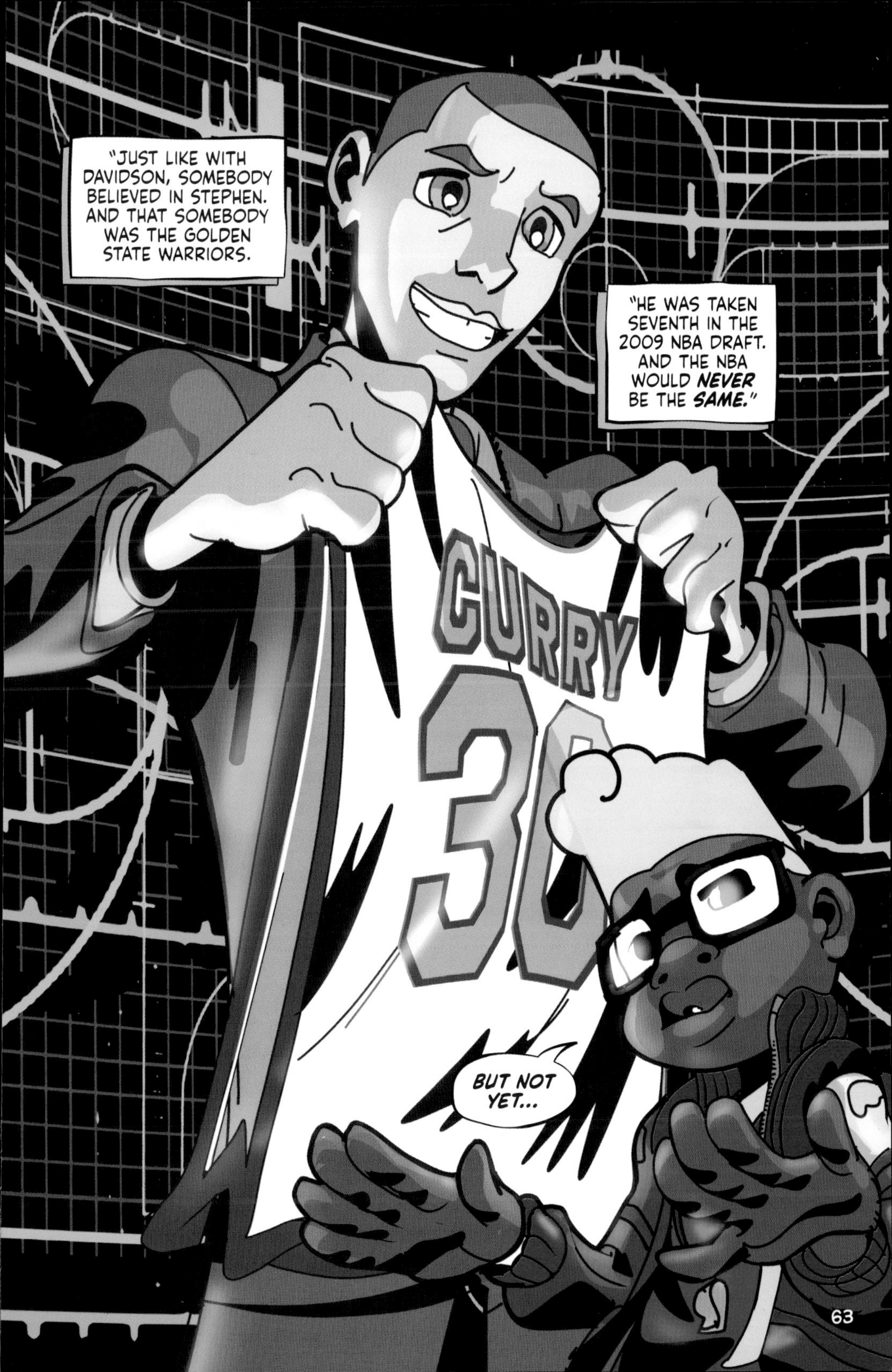
"JUST LIKE WITH DAVIDSON, SOMEBODY BELIEVED IN STEPHEN. AND THAT SOMEBODY WAS THE GOLDEN STATE WARRIORS.
"HE WAS TAKEN SEVENTH IN THE 2009 NBA DRAFT. AND THE NBA WOULD *NEVER* BE THE *SAME*."
CURRY
30
BUT NOT YET...

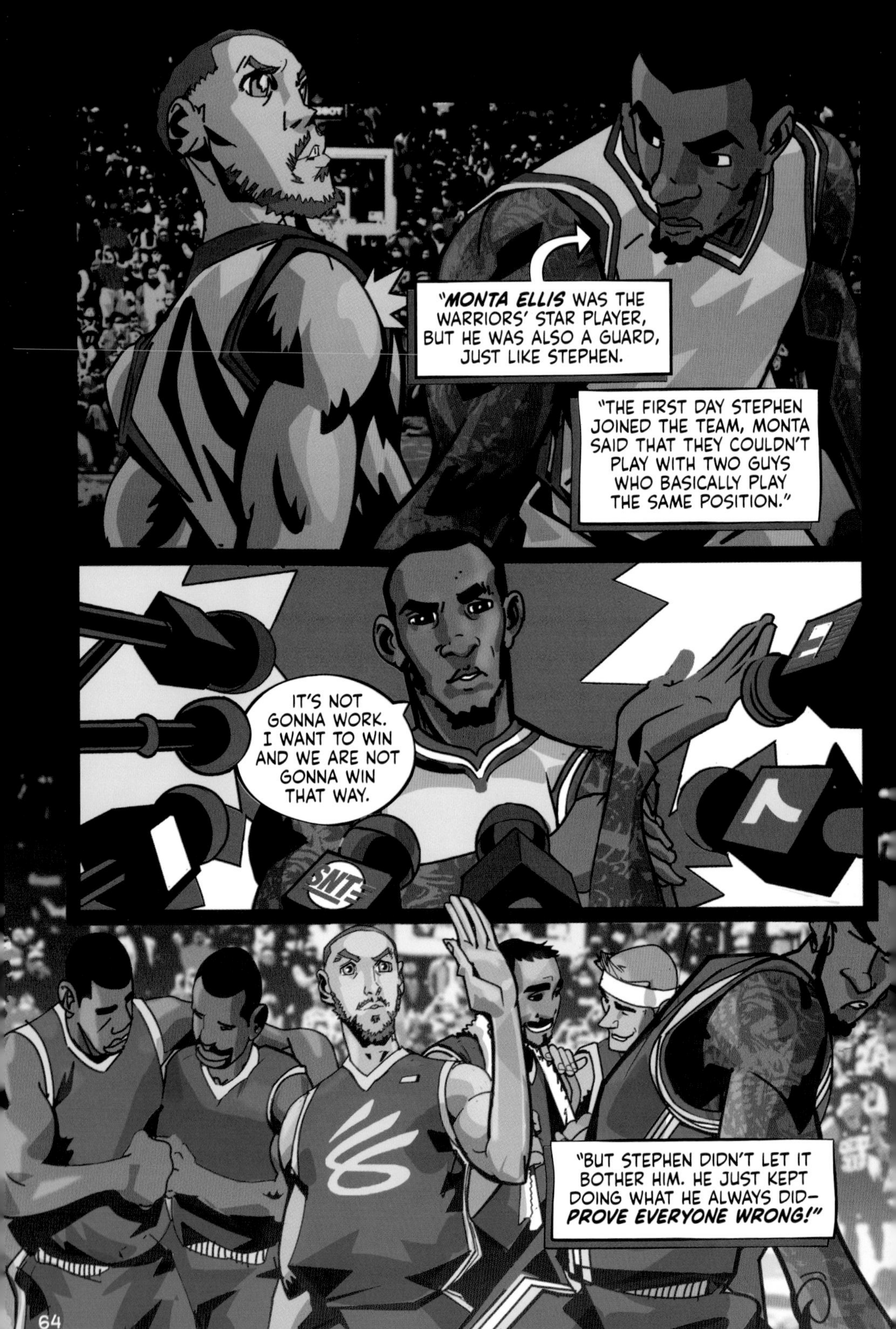
"MONTA ELLIS WAS THE WARRIORS' STAR PLAYER, BUT HE WAS ALSO A GUARD, JUST LIKE STEPHEN.
"THE FIRST DAY STEPHEN JOINED THE TEAM, MONTA SAID THAT THEY COULDN'T PLAY WITH TWO GUYS WHO BASICALLY PLAY THE SAME POSITION."
IT'S NOT GONNA WORK. I WANT TO WIN AND WE ARE NOT GONNA WIN THAT WAY.
SNTE
"BUT STEPHEN DIDN'T LET IT BOTHER HIM. HE JUST KEPT DOING WHAT HE ALWAYS DID— PROVE EVERYONE WRONG!"

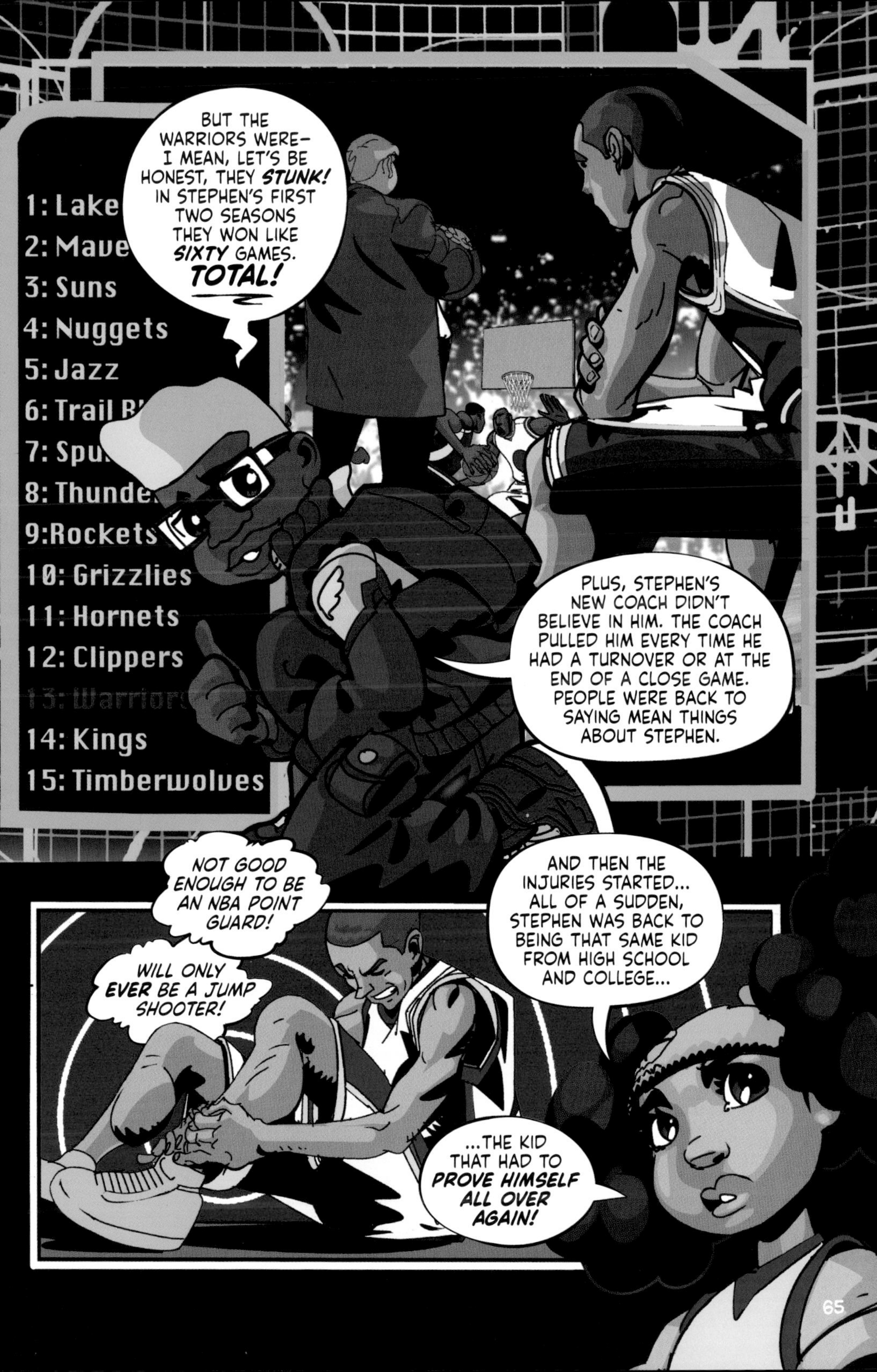

BUT THE WARRIORS WERE— I MEAN, LET'S BE HONEST, THEY STUNK! IN STEPHEN'S FIRST TWO SEASONS THEY WON LIKE SIXTY GAMES. TOTAL!
1: Lake
2: Mave
3: Suns
4: Nuggets
5: Jazz
6: Trail Bl
7: Spu
8: Thunde
9:Rockets
10: Grizzlies
11: Hornets
12: Clippers
13: Warriors
14: Kings
15: Timberwolves
PLUS, STEPHEN'S NEW COACH DIDN'T BELIEVE IN HIM. THE COACH PULLED HIM EVERY TIME HE HAD A TURNOVER OR AT THE END OF A CLOSE GAME. PEOPLE WERE BACK TO SAYING MEAN THINGS ABOUT STEPHEN.
NOT GOOD ENOUGH TO BE AN NBA POINT GUARD!
WILL ONLY EVER BE A JUMP SHOOTER!
AND THEN THE INJURIES STARTED... ALL OF A SUDDEN, STEPHEN WAS BACK TO BEING THAT SAME KID FROM HIGH SCHOOL AND COLLEGE...
...THE KID THAT HAD TO PROVE HIMSELF ALL OVER AGAIN!

CHAPTER
TEN

THE ANKLES!

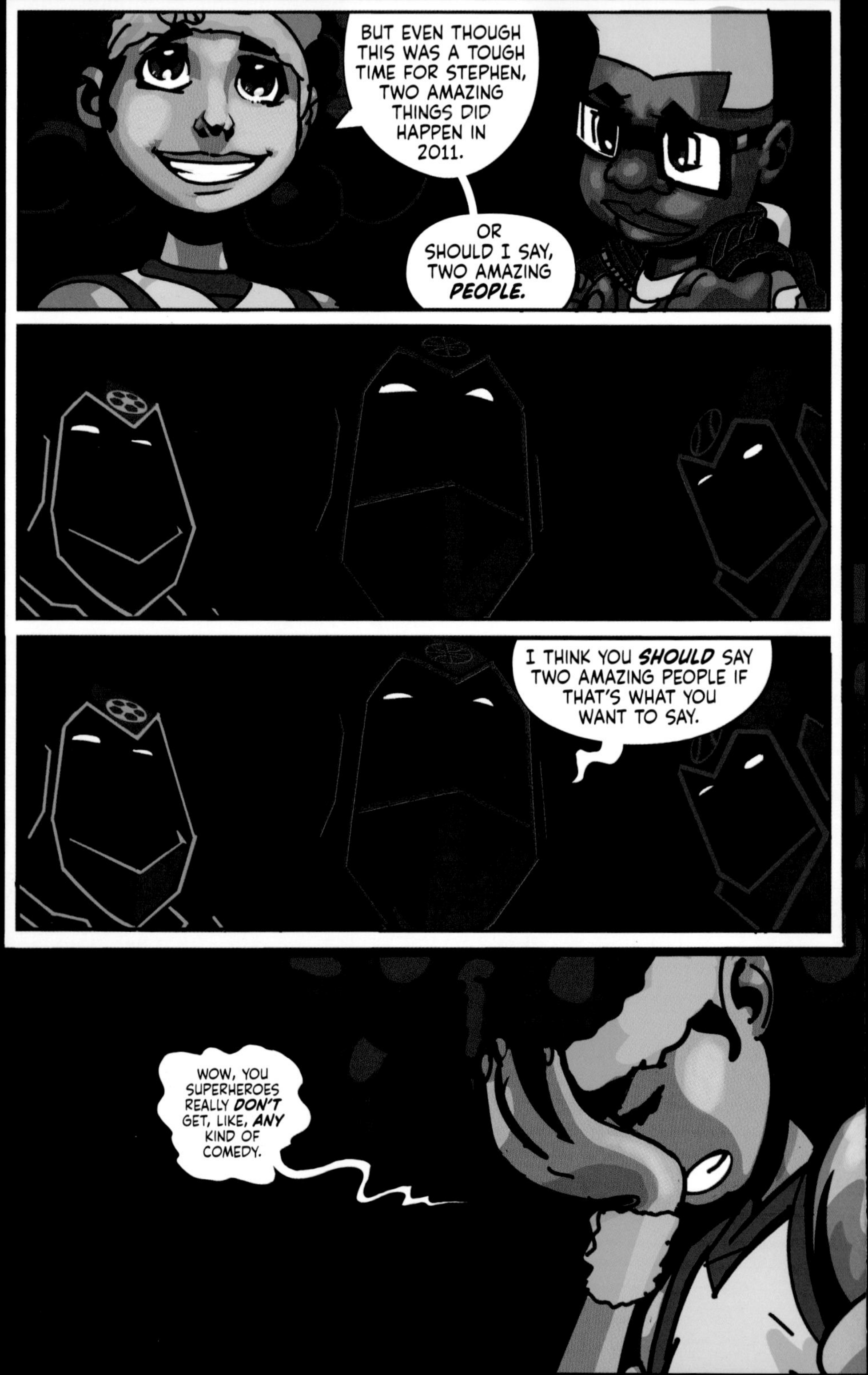
BUT EVEN THOUGH THIS WAS A TOUGH TIME FOR STEPHEN, TWO AMAZING THINGS DID HAPPEN IN 2011.
OR SHOULD I SAY, TWO AMAZING *PEOPLE.*
I THINK YOU *SHOULD* SAY TWO AMAZING PEOPLE IF THAT'S WHAT YOU WANT TO SAY.
WOW, YOU SUPERHEROES REALLY *DON'T* GET, LIKE, *ANY* KIND OF COMEDY.

CHAPTER ELEVEN

AYESHA AND STEPHEN!

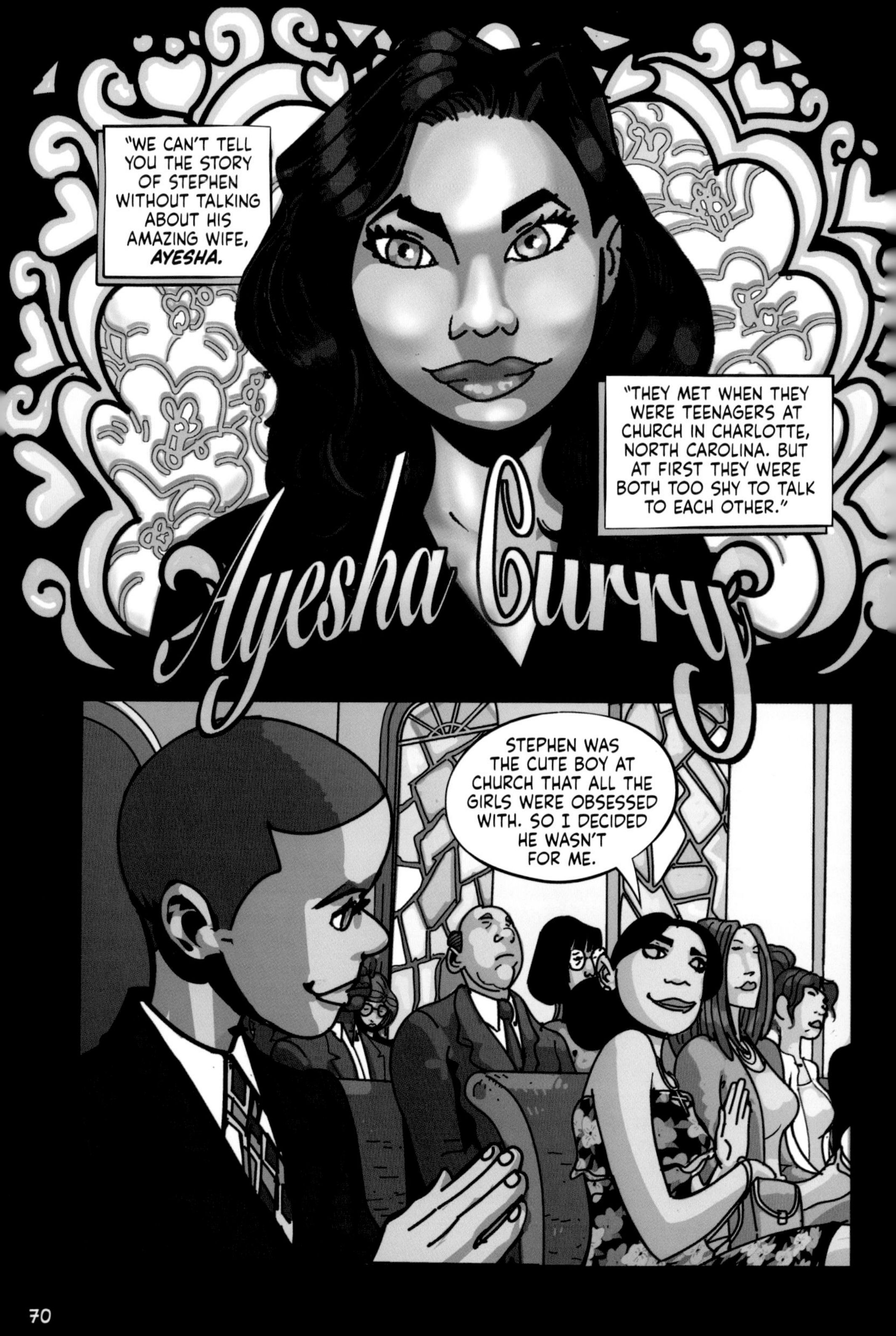
"WE CAN'T TELL YOU THE STORY OF STEPHEN WITHOUT TALKING ABOUT HIS AMAZING WIFE, AYESHA.
"THEY MET WHEN THEY WERE TEENAGERS AT CHURCH IN CHARLOTTE, NORTH CAROLINA. BUT AT FIRST THEY WERE BOTH TOO SHY TO TALK TO EACH OTHER."
Ayesha Curry
STEPHEN WAS THE CUTE BOY AT CHURCH THAT ALL THE GIRLS WERE OBSESSED WITH. SO I DECIDED HE WASN'T FOR ME.

CHAPTER TWELVE

THE PROMISED LAND

"THE SEASON WAS MAGICAL FOR STEPHEN AND HIS TEAM. HE WON HIS FIRST MVP AWARD AND HIS SPEECH WAS *SO* AWESOME."

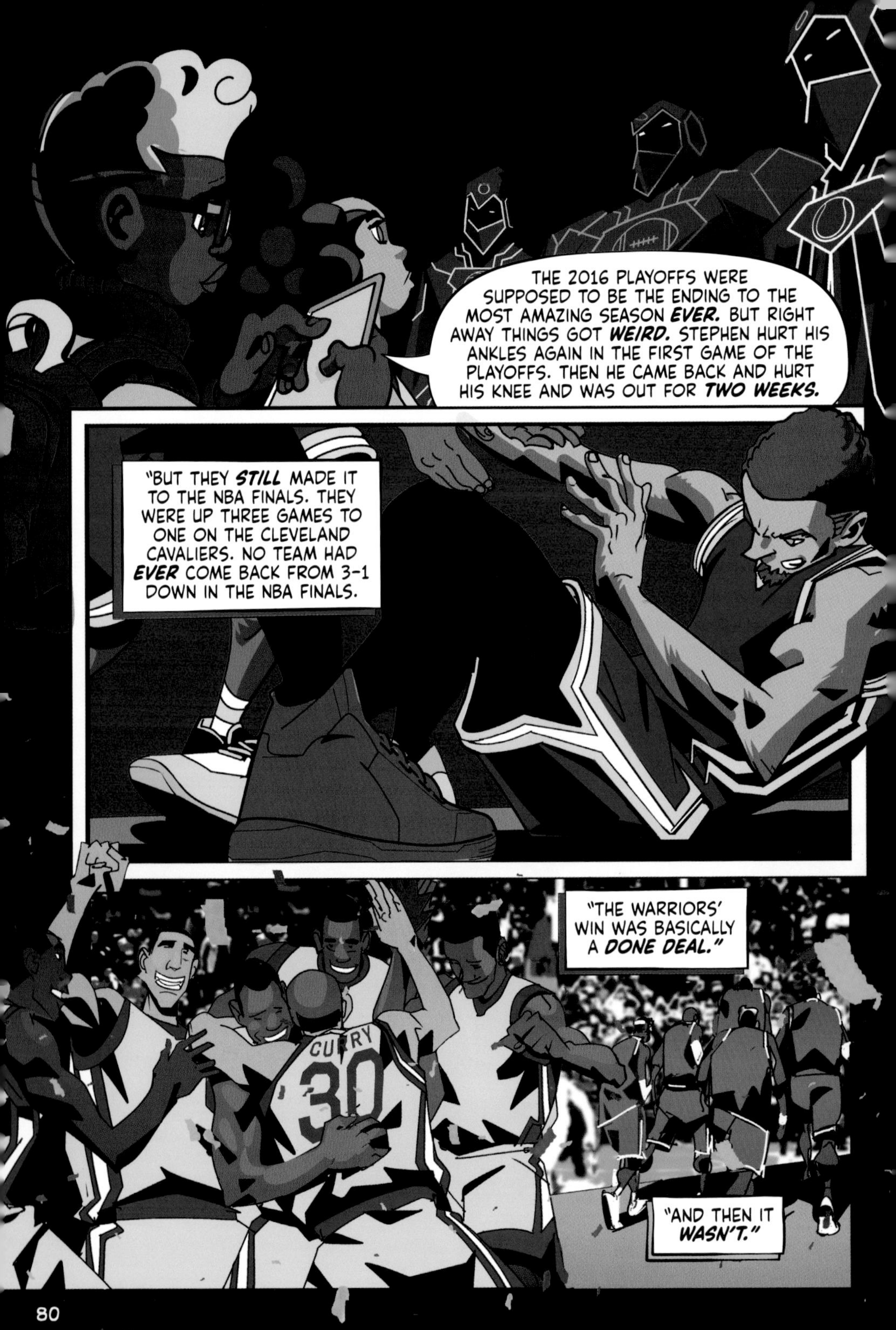
THE 2016 PLAYOFFS WERE SUPPOSED TO BE THE ENDING TO THE MOST AMAZING SEASON ***EVER.*** BUT RIGHT AWAY THINGS GOT ***WEIRD.*** STEPHEN HURT HIS ANKLES AGAIN IN THE FIRST GAME OF THE PLAYOFFS. THEN HE CAME BACK AND HURT HIS KNEE AND WAS OUT FOR ***TWO WEEKS.***
"BUT THEY ***STILL*** MADE IT TO THE NBA FINALS. THEY WERE UP THREE GAMES TO ONE ON THE CLEVELAND CAVALIERS. NO TEAM HAD ***EVER*** COME BACK FROM 3-1 DOWN IN THE NBA FINALS.
CURRY
30
"THE WARRIORS' WIN WAS BASICALLY A ***DONE DEAL.***"
"AND THEN IT ***WASN'T.***"

CHAPTER THIRTEEN

SUPERFRIENDS

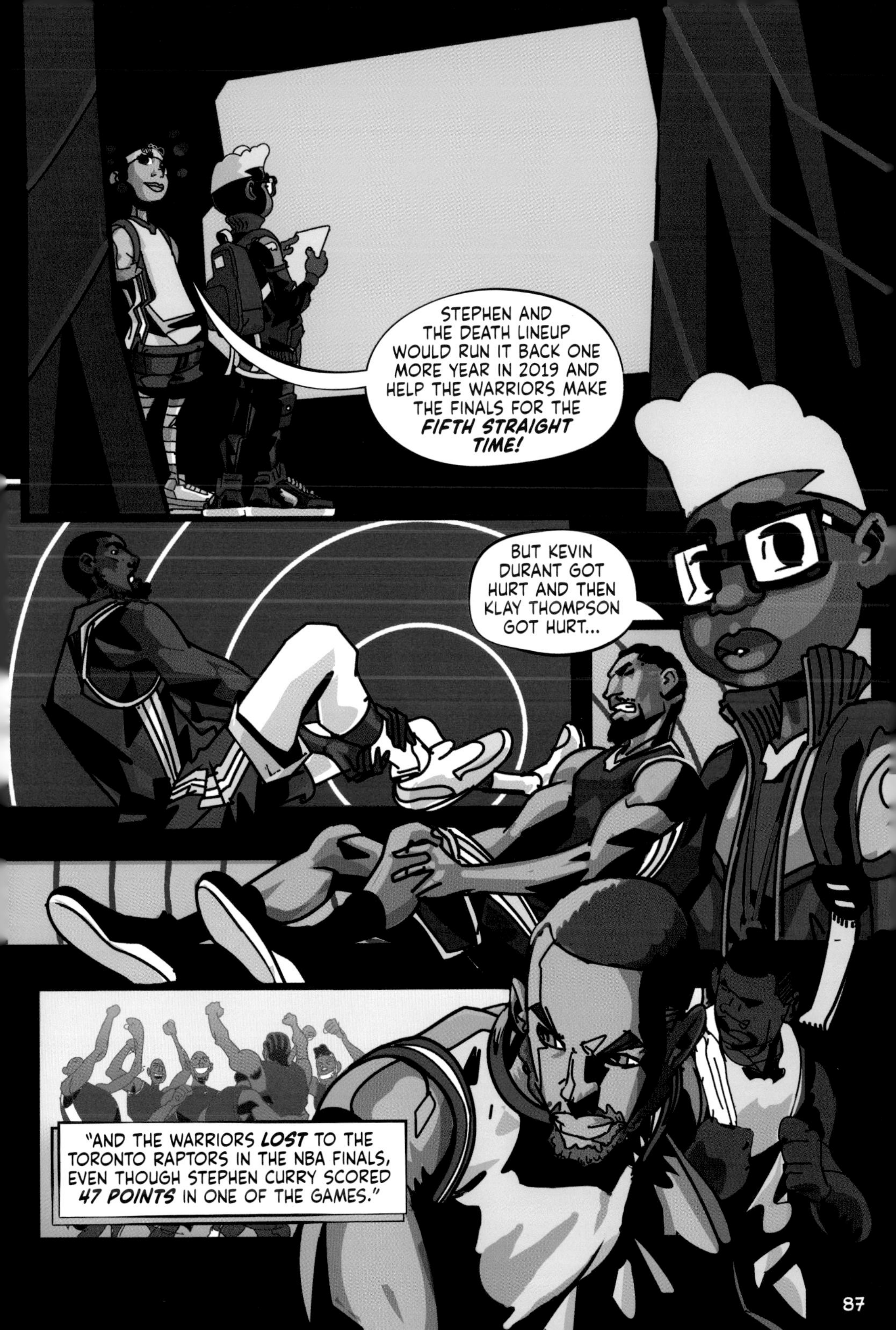
STEPHEN AND THE DEATH LINEUP WOULD RUN IT BACK ONE MORE YEAR IN 2019 AND HELP THE WARRIORS MAKE THE FINALS FOR THE ***FIFTH STRAIGHT TIME!***
BUT KEVIN DURANT GOT HURT AND THEN KLAY THOMPSON GOT HURT...
"AND THE WARRIORS ***LOST*** TO THE TORONTO RAPTORS IN THE NBA FINALS, EVEN THOUGH STEPHEN CURRY SCORED ***47 POINTS*** IN ONE OF THE GAMES."

CHAPTER
FOURTEEN

THE LOST YEARS AND
BACK TO THE MOUNTAINTOP

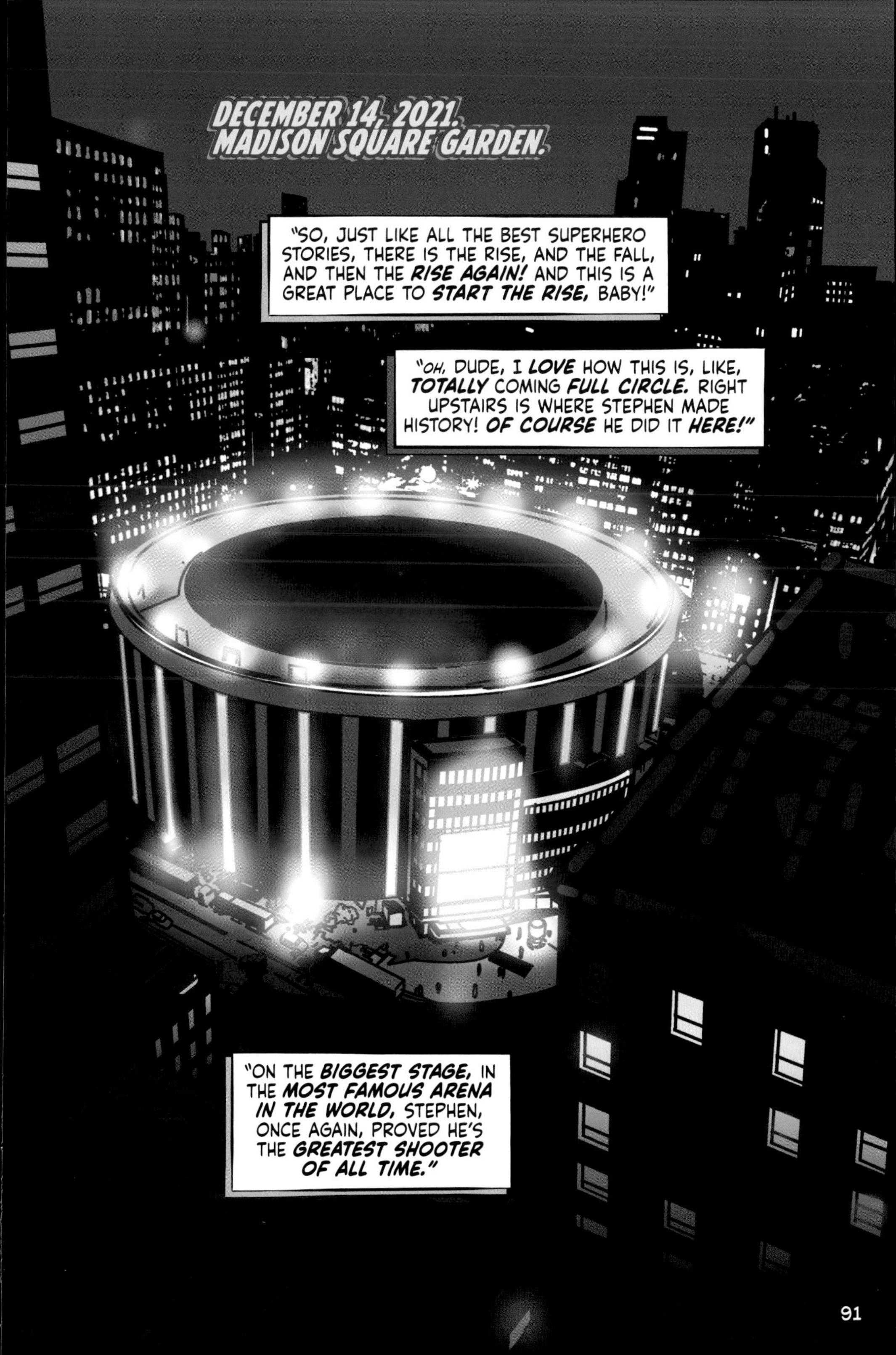
DECEMBER 14, 2021.
MADISON SQUARE GARDEN.
"SO, JUST LIKE ALL THE BEST SUPERHERO STORIES, THERE IS THE RISE, AND THE FALL, AND THEN THE RISE AGAIN! AND THIS IS A GREAT PLACE TO START THE RISE, BABY!"
"OH, DUDE, I LOVE HOW THIS IS, LIKE, TOTALLY COMING FULL CIRCLE. RIGHT UPSTAIRS IS WHERE STEPHEN MADE HISTORY! OF COURSE HE DID IT HERE!"
"ON THE BIGGEST STAGE, IN THE MOST FAMOUS ARENA IN THE WORLD, STEPHEN, ONCE AGAIN, PROVED HE'S THE GREATEST SHOOTER OF ALL TIME."

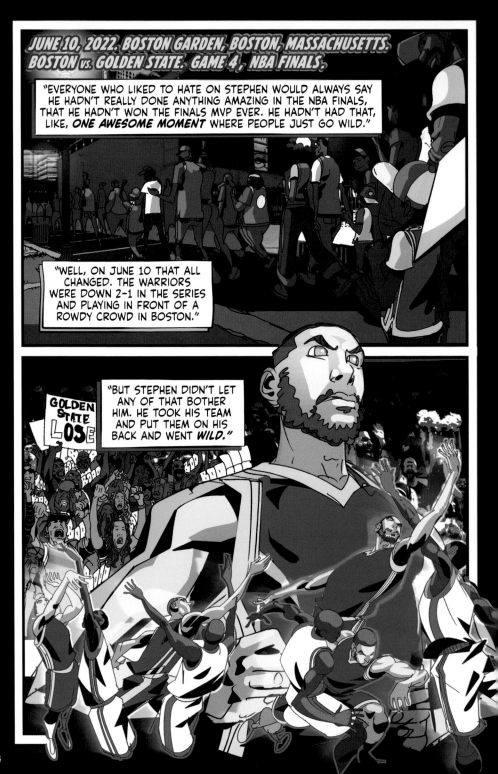

JUNE 10, 2022. BOSTON GARDEN, BOSTON, MASSACHUSETTS. BOSTON vs. GOLDEN STATE. GAME 4, NBA FINALS.

"EVERYONE WHO LIKED TO HATE ON STEPHEN WOULD ALWAYS SAY HE HADN'T REALLY DONE ANYTHING AMAZING IN THE NBA FINALS, THAT HE HADN'T WON THE FINALS MVP EVER. HE HADN'T HAD THAT, LIKE, *ONE AWESOME MOMENT* WHERE PEOPLE JUST GO WILD."

"WELL, ON JUNE 10 THAT ALL CHANGED. THE WARRIORS WERE DOWN 2–1 IN THE SERIES AND PLAYING IN FRONT OF A ROWDY CROWD IN BOSTON."

GOLDEN STATE LOSE

"BUT STEPHEN DIDN'T LET ANY OF THAT BOTHER HIM. HE TOOK HIS TEAM AND PUT THEM ON HIS BACK AND WENT *WILD*."

94

CHAPTER
FIFTEEN

DECISION TIME

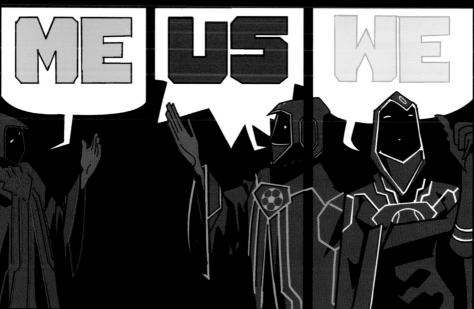

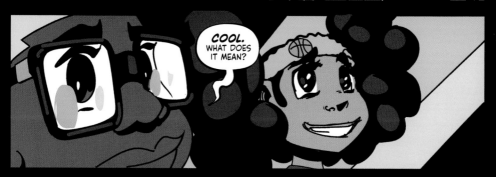

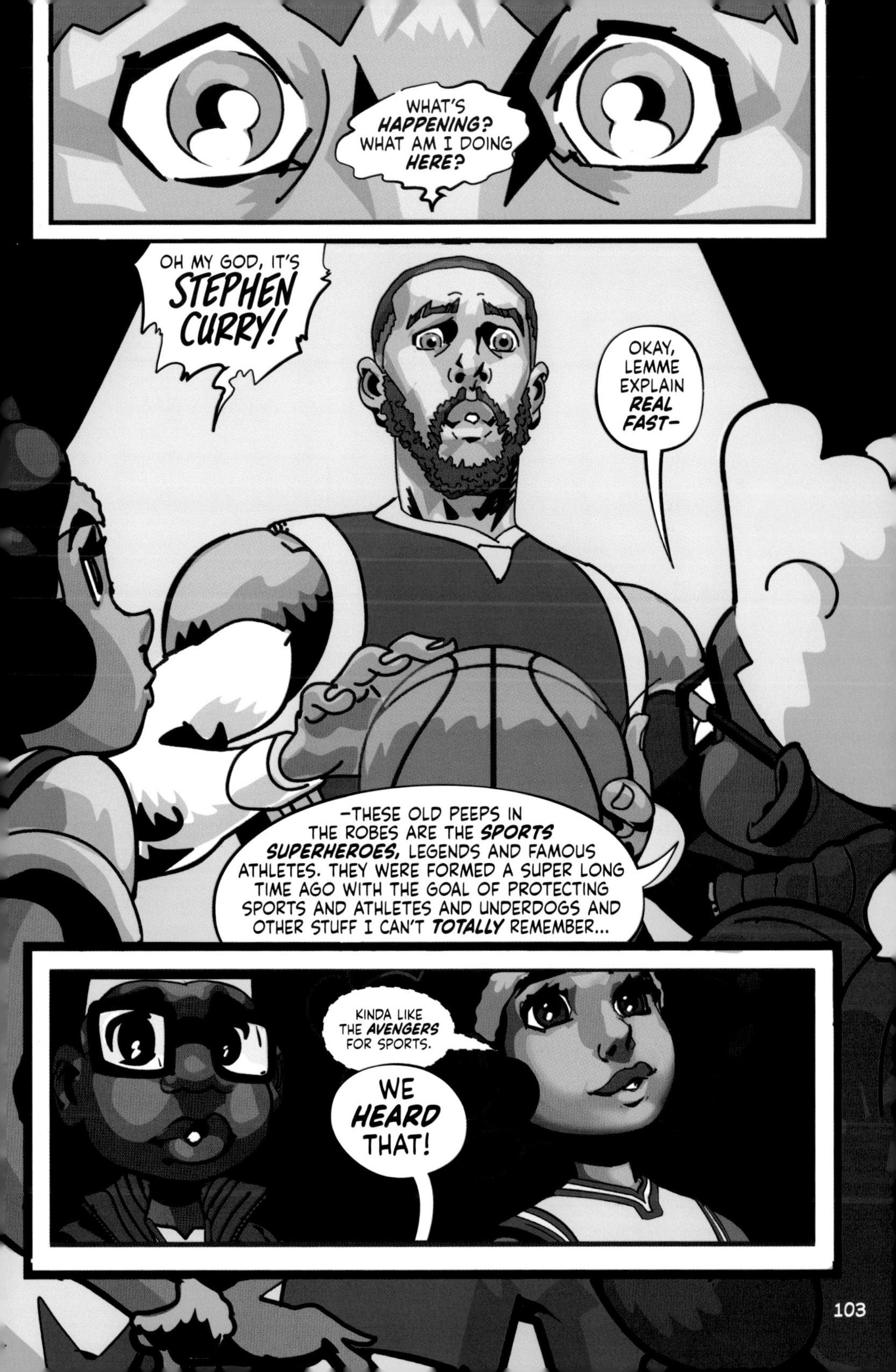
WHAT'S HAPPENING? WHAT AM I DOING HERE?
OH MY GOD, IT'S STEPHEN CURRY!
OKAY, LEMME EXPLAIN REAL FAST–
–THESE OLD PEEPS IN THE ROBES ARE THE SPORTS SUPERHEROES, LEGENDS AND FAMOUS ATHLETES. THEY WERE FORMED A SUPER LONG TIME AGO WITH THE GOAL OF PROTECTING SPORTS AND ATHLETES AND UNDERDOGS AND OTHER STUFF I CAN'T TOTALLY REMEMBER...
KINDA LIKE THE AVENGERS FOR SPORTS.
WE HEARD THAT!

105

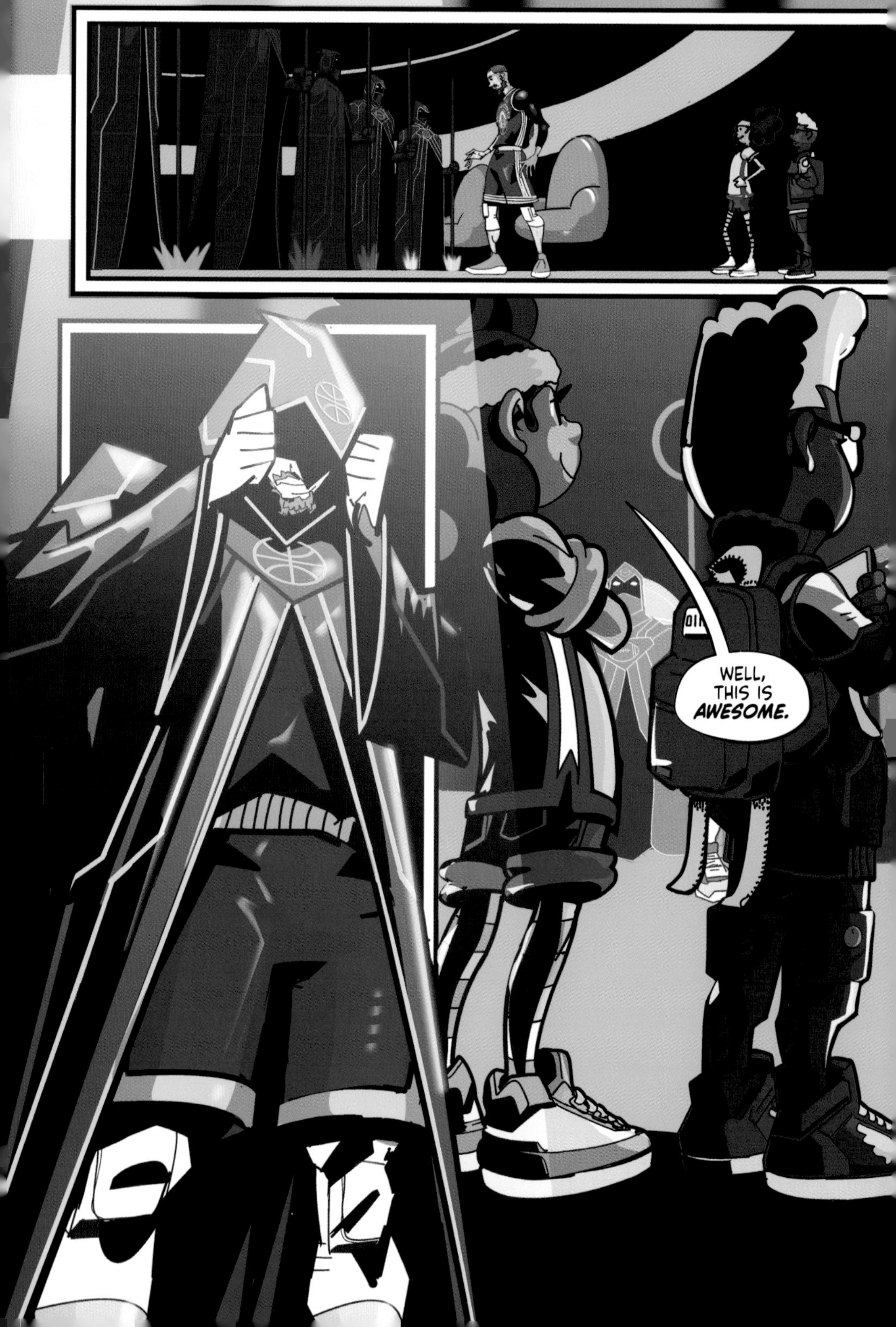
WELL, THIS IS AWESOME.

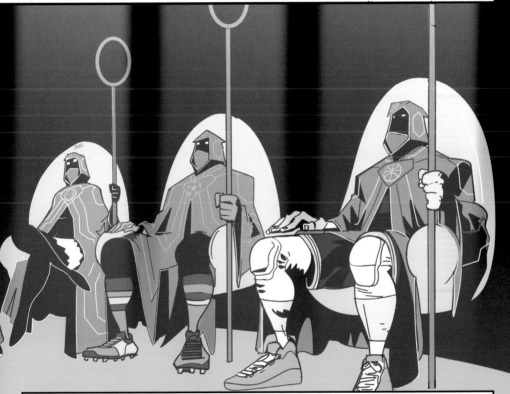

WHAT HAPPENS NEX—